BOUNDLESS: THE PATH TO DIVINE POSSIBILITIES

Activating Each Day in Prophetic Power

David S. Philemon

Royal Diadem Publishing Inc.

Dedication

To the Almighty God, my foundation and ever-present help. I am grateful for Your boundless love and grace that sustain me daily. And to my mentor in ministry, Rev. George Izunwa, whose steadfast commitment to the call of God has deeply impacted my life. Your guidance and support have been invaluable, encouraging me to walk boldly in the path God has set before me. Thank you for your example and your heart for the Kingdom.

ACKNOWLEDGMENTS

This book would not have been possible without the unwavering support, dedication, and talent of an extraordinary team. My deepest gratitude goes to each of you for your contributions, insights, and encouragement throughout this journey.

First and foremost, thank you to Rev. Mimi Philemon my dear wife, Rev. Shina Gentry, and and my assistant pastor Rev. Bright Amudoaghan for your incredible effort, encouragement, and belief in this project. Your support has been instrumental in bringing this vision to life.

To the dedicated leaders of Royal Diadem Publishing, Ide Imogie and Kishawna Bailey, I am immensely grateful for your belief in this project from the very beginning and for investing your time and energy into its development. Your creativity, dedication, and expertise have been the backbone of this endeavor.

I am especially grateful to the Royal Diadem Publishing team— Beulah Orogun, Emmanuella Ben-Eboh, Doyinsade Awodele, Kim Matthews, and Shante Gill, for your meticulous attention to detail, refining every page and ensuring that each word reflects our vision.

A heartfelt thank you to my family, friends, and colleagues whose unwavering support and belief in this project gave me the courage and strength to see it through.

Finally, thank you to all the readers and supporters who make this work meaningful. I am humbled and honored to share this journey with each of you.

With all my gratitude,
David Philemon

CONTENTS

FROM APOSTLE DR. DAVID PHILEMON

INTRODUCTION

The Power Of Activation

E very day holds untapped potential, a unique opportunity to encounter divine possibilities that can transform our lives. But too often, we walk through life without realizing the power we have to activate those possibilities. Through spiritual activation, we can align ourselves with God's purpose and unlock the supernatural realm, allowing us to experience His abundance, guidance, and favor.

This book is written for those who desire to live a life of spiritual empowerment, for those who are tired of walking in uncertainty and want to step into God's prophetic plan. Each day presents a new chance to partner with the Holy Spirit, to activate the divine presence in our lives, and to walk in a realm of endless possibilities.

Activation isn't just a religious practice; it's a lifestyle of faith. It's the intentional decision to begin each day by engaging with God, drawing on His wisdom, and positioning ourselves to receive from Him. When we do this, we invite God to take charge of our day, and as a result, we experience breakthroughs, favors, and miracles.

In this book, I'll share with you not only the principles of daily activation but also the testimonies of those who have seen incredible transformations by applying these truths. You will learn how to stay patient in God's presence, master spiritual details, and walk in the limitless possibilities that God offers through His prophetic insight.

As you read, I encourage you to open your heart and mind to receive. This is not just another book. This is a call to action, a call to live your life fully empowered by God. The prophetic realm is not distant; it's available to you right here, right now. You simply need to activate it.

Prepare yourself for a journey of spiritual discovery. Together, we will unlock the secrets to activating each day with the power of God and step into a life where miracles, breakthroughs, and divine favor are your everyday reality.

CHAPTER 1

EMPOWERING YOUR LIFE BY ACTIVATING YOUR DAY

E ach day is a blank canvas, waiting to be painted with the colors of divine purpose. The choices we make from the moment we wake up determine the spiritual tone of our day. To live a life empowered by God, it's crucial to start each day by activating His presence and aligning with His will.

What is Daily Spiritual Activation?

What does it mean to activate your day spiritually? It's more than a routine prayer or devotional; it's a deliberate and conscious engagement with the supernatural realm, allowing the Holy Spirit to lead and guide every moment. Activation is the key to unlocking God's power and purpose for your life each day.

Many believers often go through the motions of prayer without understanding its significance in daily living. They check off a morning prayer from their to-do list but forget that true spiritual activation requires depth, patience, and focus. It's not about how many minutes we spend, but the quality of our engagement with God.

Imagine starting your day by sitting in the presence of the Creator, the One who knows the end from the beginning. He has prepared blessings, breakthroughs, and opportunities for you. But to access them, you must be spiritually alert and activated. Daily activation is the doorway through which you enter into God's prophetic agenda for your life.

The Power of Alignment

One of the key aspects of daily activation is alignment with God's will. Many people live in frustration because they operate outside of God's plan, trying to solve problems in their own strength. They wonder why things aren't working, unaware that the answer lies in aligning their thoughts, words, and actions with what God desires for them that day.

When you activate your day through prayer, worship, and meditation on the Word of God, you are essentially aligning yourself with heaven's agenda. You become attuned to the voice of the Holy Spirit, who will guide you throughout the day. This alignment brings clarity to your decisions and fills you with a sense of peace, even when challenges arise.

Jesus exemplified this alignment during His earthly ministry. Every morning, He would retreat to solitary places to pray and seek the Father's will. It was through this daily activation that He was able to perform miracles, teach with authority, and fulfill His divine mission. His life shows us that without spiritual alignment, we may miss the divine opportunities that await us.

Activating the Prophetic Realm

Daily spiritual activation is not just about personal alignment; it also opens the door to prophetic insight. The prophetic realm is one where God reveals His plans and purposes to His children. When you activate your day, you are positioning yourself to receive prophetic guidance.

The prophetic realm is like a radio frequency. You can only hear it when you're tuned in. Activating your day through prayer and worship is like turning the dial to the right frequency, where God's voice becomes clear. You will begin to hear Him speak concerning your day, your family, your work, and even the challenges ahead.

Through this prophetic activation, you gain an advantage over the natural realm. You will know how to handle situations before they arise because God will reveal to you the hidden things. As the Bible says in Amos 3:7, "Surely the Lord God does nothing unless He reveals His secret to His servants the prophets." When you activate your day, you become a recipient of God's secrets, and this knowledge equips you to live victoriously.

Living with Intentionality

A spiritually activated life is one lived with intentionality. When you activate your day, you're no longer wandering through life, hoping for good things to happen by chance. Instead, you are stepping into each day with purpose and expectation, knowing that God has gone before you to prepare the way.

Living intentionally means that you approach every task, relationship, and opportunity with the mindset of fulfilling God's will. Your work becomes an act of worship, your interactions are filled with grace, and your challenges are met with faith. You stop living reactively, responding to crises as they come, and start living proactively, shaping your environment through spiritual activation.

In Proverbs 16:3, we are told to "commit our works to the Lord, and our thoughts will be established." This is the essence of spiritual activation. When you commit your day to God, He will establish your thoughts and direct your steps. There is no greater empowerment than knowing that the Creator of the universe is orchestrating your life.

Overcoming Distractions in the Morning

One of the biggest challenges to daily spiritual activation is distraction. The enemy knows the power of starting your day with God, so he often tries to fill your mind with concerns, tasks, and unnecessary noise to keep you from focusing. Emails, social media, and even worry about the day ahead can cloud your spiritual vision, making it hard to connect with God.

But when you prioritize spiritual activation, you are making a statement that God comes first. Before you check your phone, before you rush into the busyness of life, take time to sit at the feet of Jesus. Give Him your full attention, and you will find that the distractions lose their power.

Set a routine that minimizes distractions in the morning. Find a quiet place, free from interruptions, where you can spend quality time with God. This space becomes sacred, where heaven and earth meet, and you are empowered for the day ahead.

Engaging with God Through Worship and Prayer

Worship and prayer are the foundational tools of spiritual activation. Worship opens the heavens and brings you into the presence of God, where you can experience His glory and power. Prayer, on the other hand, is your means of communication with God, where you pour out your heart and receive His instructions.

When you combine worship and prayer in your daily routine, you are creating an atmosphere where the Holy Spirit can move freely. Worship shifts your focus from yourself to God, reminding you of His greatness. Prayer then becomes more than a list of requests; it becomes a conversation with the One who holds all power.

In John 4:24, Jesus said, "God is Spirit, and those who worship Him must worship in spirit and truth." This is the heart of daily activation, that is, coming before God with a sincere heart, worshiping Him in spirit and truth, and allowing His Spirit to lead you throughout the day.

The Role of Scripture in Daily Activation

No spiritual activation is complete without the word of God. The

Bible is our guide, our roadmap for life. It is through Scripture that we gain understanding, wisdom, and direction for our day. When you activate your day, make sure to meditate on the Word of God, letting it shape your thoughts and actions.

Psalm 119:105 says, "Your word is a lamp to my feet and a light to my path." The Word of God illuminates the way forward, helping you navigate life's challenges with confidence. When you start your day by meditating on Scripture, you are equipping yourself with the spiritual tools needed to overcome any obstacle.

Daily activation through the word transforms your mind, renews your spirit, and strengthens your faith. It becomes the solid foundation upon which you build your day, giving you the assurance that no matter what comes, God's Word will see you through.

The Importance of Aligning with God's Will Daily

Aligning with God's will is at the core of daily spiritual activation. It is a critical step that allows us to experience His fullness and live in harmony with His divine plan. Without alignment, even the most well-intentioned actions may fall short of God's purpose. To walk in divine power, wisdom, and favor, we must first align ourselves with God's will every single day.

Why Alignment Matters

Alignment with God's will is more than just following a set of rules or principles. It's about entering into a relationship where we are constantly seeking His heart and direction for our lives. Many times, believers make decisions based on their own understanding or desires, only to realize later that they have missed God's best for them. When we live outside of God's will, we limit what He can do in and through us.

The Bible reminds us in Proverbs 3:5-6 to "trust in the Lord with all your heart, and lean not on your own understanding; in all your ways acknowledge Him, and He shall direct your paths." This scripture emphasizes the need to submit to God in all aspects of life, allowing Him to guide our steps. When we acknowledge Him, we position ourselves to receive divine direction that leads to success, peace, and fulfillment.

Living Outside of Alignment

Living outside of alignment with God's will can be likened to driving a car with misaligned wheels. You may be moving forward, but the journey is rough, and the car will likely veer off course. Just as a vehicle with misaligned wheels can wear down its tires and components prematurely, living out of sync with God can lead to frustration, confusion, and wasted time in our lives. We may accomplish many things, but they are often not in the way God intended for us.

When we operate outside of God's alignment, we become vulnerable to making decisions driven by fear, pressure, or a desire for control. For example, in 1 Samuel 13, we see King Saul's impulsiveness when he offered sacrifices to God without waiting for the prophet Samuel. This decision was born out of fear and pressure from his army, which was becoming anxious as they faced the Philistines. Saul's impatience resulted in God rejecting him as king, demonstrating that acting outside of God's timing and alignment can lead to dire consequences.

Another illustration can be found in Proverbs 14:12, which states, "There is a way that seems right to a man, but its end is the way of death." This verse reminds us that our own understanding and desires can mislead us. For instance, someone might pursue a lucrative job opportunity that appears promising but leads to ethical dilemmas or a lack of fulfillment. When our choices are made outside of God's alignment, we risk falling into paths that lead to exhaustion and disappointment.

The key to living in alignment with God's will is to seek His guidance and wisdom actively. In James 1:5, we are encouraged to ask God for wisdom, assuring us that He gives generously to all without finding fault. Consider the example of Solomon, who, when given the opportunity to request anything from God, chose wisdom above all else (1 Kings 3:5-14). As a result, his reign was marked by peace and prosperity. This demonstrates how aligning ourselves with God's purposes can lead to divine favor and success.

At the same time, when we rush into situations without consulting God, we often find ourselves entangled in deeper problems. For instance, the Israelites' desire for a king, as documented in 1 Samuel 8, led to their demand for Saul as their ruler. Despite God's warnings about the implications of having a human king, they insisted. Their choice ultimately led to oppression and strife, showcasing how decisions made outside of God's alignment can result in turmoil.

In contrast, when we are aligned with God's will, even the most challenging circumstances become manageable. For instance, in Philippians 4:6-7, Paul encourages us not to be anxious about anything but to present our requests to God. When we do this, the peace of God guards our hearts and minds. This peace is not contingent on our external circumstances but is rooted in our alignment with God's purposes.

A powerful example of peace in alignment can be seen in the life of Jesus. In Matthew 26:39, as He faced the impending crucifixion, Jesus prayed, "Not as I will, but as You will." His submission to God's plan, despite the pain it entailed, brought about the ultimate victory over sin and death. Jesus exemplified that true alignment comes from resting in God's will, allowing us to experience peace even in the face of trials.

Living in alignment with God also allows us to rest in His ability rather than striving in our strength. In Matthew 11:28-30, Jesus invites those who are weary and burdened to come to Him for rest. He promises to take on our burdens and teach us His ways, emphasizing that His yoke is easy, and His burden is light. This passage illustrates that alignment with God leads to rest and renewal.

Consider the story of Moses in Exodus 3-4, where God calls him to lead the Israelites out of Egypt. Initially, Moses feels inadequate and resistant, questioning God's choice of him. However, as he submits to God's plan, he discovers that God equips those He calls. Moses experienced God's miraculous power through signs and wonders, allowing him to lead the Israelites toward freedom. His alignment with God's will not only transformed his life but also the destiny of an entire nation.

Life will inevitably present challenges, but when we align ourselves with God, we can navigate these trials with grace. The story of Daniel in Daniel 6 serves as a prime example. When faced with the threat of being thrown into the lion's den for praying to God, Daniel remained steadfast in his commitment to align with God's will, despite the dangers. His faithfulness led to miraculous deliverance, demonstrating that God honors those who remain aligned with Him.

Similarly, in Romans 8:28, we are assured that "all things work together for good to those who love God, to those who are called according to His purpose." This verse encapsulates the essence of living in alignment with God. When we surrender our plans and desires to Him, we can trust that even the difficult moments will ultimately contribute to our good and His glory.

The Daily Act of Submission

Aligning with God's will is not a one-time decision; it is a daily act of submission. Each morning, as we activate our day, we must consciously surrender our plans, desires, and agendas to Him. It's easy to wake up and immediately focus on what we want to accomplish or how we think the day should go. But to align with God's will, we must first ask Him what He wants.

Jesus taught this in the Lord's Prayer when He said, "Your kingdom come, Your will be done on earth as it is in heaven" (Matthew 6:10). This simple yet powerful phrase reflects a heart of submission to God's will. Before we ask for anything, we are to seek His kingdom and His will above all else.

Each day, as we surrender to God, we invite Him to take control. We acknowledge that He knows better than we do, and that His plans for us are good. This act of submission doesn't mean we abandon our desires or dreams; it means we trust God to fulfill them in His way and in His time. When we do this, we align with the flow of His grace and favor.

Recognizing God's Will for the Day

One of the greatest challenges for many believers is discerning what God's will is for them each day. How do we know what He wants us to do, and how can we be sure we are on the right path?

The first key to recognizing God's will is through His Word. The Bible is God's revealed will for all believers. When we spend time reading and meditating on Scripture, we align our hearts with His. The more familiar we are with His Word, the more we will recognize His voice and guidance in our daily lives.

Psalm 119:105 says, "Your word is a lamp to my feet and a light to my path." This means that God's Word provides clarity and direction for each step we take. When we begin our day by meditating on His promises, commandments, and instructions, we are setting ourselves up to walk in His will. The Bible becomes a filter through which we can measure our thoughts, actions, and decisions.

Prayer is another essential tool for discerning God's will. Prayer is not just about presenting our needs to God; it's also about listening for His voice. As we spend time in prayer, we create space for the Holy Spirit to speak to us, guiding our decisions and actions. Sometimes, God's will is revealed through a still, small voice, while at other times, it comes through an undeniable prompting or confirmation.

In addition to Scripture and prayer, we also discern God's will through the peace of the Holy Spirit. Colossians 3:15 encourages us to "let the peace of God rule in your hearts." When we are walking in alignment with God's will, there is a peace that accompanies our decisions. If you are facing a situation and feel anxious, restless, or uneasy, it may be a sign that you need to pause and seek God's direction.

Staying in Alignment Throughout the Day

Aligning with God's will is not limited to the moments of prayer in the morning. It's a continual process that lasts throughout the day. As you go about your activities, it's important to stay sensitive to the Holy Spirit's leading. God may give you an initial direction in the morning, but as the day unfolds, He may adjust your course based on circumstances or new revelations.

Staying in alignment requires humility and a willingness to change plans when necessary. Sometimes we can get so caught up in what we think should happen that we miss God's subtle promptings. However, when we remain flexible and open to His leading, we allow Him to redirect us as needed.

James 4:13-15 speaks to this attitude of flexibility: "Come now, you who say, 'Today or tomorrow we will go to such and such a city, spend a year there, buy and sell, and make a profit'; whereas you do not know what will happen tomorrow. For what is your life? It is even a vapor that appears for a little time and then vanishes away. Instead, you ought to say, 'If the Lord wills, we shall live and do this or that.'"

This passage reminds us that life is unpredictable, and only God knows what each day holds. Therefore, it's wise to submit our plans to Him continually, allowing Him to guide us in the way that is best. As we go through the day, we should be constantly checking in with God, asking, "Lord, am I still on track with Your will?"

The Blessings of Alignment

When we make it a daily practice to align with God's will, we open ourselves up to incredible blessings. First and foremost, we experience peace, peace that surpasses all understanding (Philippians 4:7). This peace comes from knowing that we are walking in step with the Creator, and that no matter what happens, He is in control.

Another blessing of alignment is divine favor. When we are in God's will, we position ourselves to receive His favor in every area of our lives. Opportunities seem to find us, doors open that we didn't expect, and provision flows from unexpected sources. This is because God delights in blessing those who are walking according to His purpose.

Psalm 84:11 promises, "For the Lord God is a sun and shield; the Lord will give grace and glory; no good thing will He withhold from those who walk uprightly." When we align with God, we are walking uprightly, and He withholds no good thing from us. This doesn't mean we won't face challenges, but it does mean that God's favor will see us through.

Lastly, alignment brings fruitfulness. When we are aligned with God's will, our efforts are fruitful and productive. We are no longer striving in vain, but we are working in partnership with God, and His power amplifies our efforts. Jesus said in John 15:5, "I am the vine, you are the branches. He who abides in Me, and I in him, bears much fruit; for without Me you can do nothing."

As we align ourselves with God each day, we become like branches connected to the vine, drawing life, strength, and purpose from Him. Our lives bear fruit—fruit that blesses others and glorifies God.

Aligning with God's will is not a passive act; it's an intentional choice we make daily. Through prayer, Scripture, and sensitivity to the Holy Spirit, we can ensure that we are walking in harmony with God's plans for our lives. As we do this, we experience peace, favor, and fruitfulness that only come from living in His divine flow.

The more we practice daily alignment, the more attuned we become to God's voice and leading. It's a journey of trust, obedience, and surrender, but the rewards are immeasurable. As you continue to activate your day, remember that alignment is key to living an empowered, victorious life in Christ.

Prophetic Insight and How It Transforms Your Life

When we speak of activating our day, one of the most profound results is gaining prophetic insight. Prophetic insight is a spiritual gift that allows us to see beyond the natural, to understand God's plans, and to navigate life with divine wisdom and foresight. It is more than just predicting the future, it's a way of living in close relationship with God, hearing His voice, and allowing Him to direct our steps in every area of life.

Prophetic insight can completely transform the way we live. It brings clarity, guidance, and empowerment, allowing us to make decisions that align with God's purpose. With prophetic insight, we no longer walk through life blindly, uncertain about what lies ahead. Instead, we move with confidence, knowing that God has given us a glimpse of what's to come and the wisdom to navigate it.

What is Prophetic Insight?

Prophetic insight is the ability to receive revelation from God about specific situations, people, or events. It is a gift that allows us to perceive things that are hidden from the natural eye. While prophecy is often associated with foretelling the future, it also includes forthtelling, speaking God's truth into the present.

In 1 Corinthians 14:3, apostle Paul explains that "he who prophesies speaks edification and exhortation and comfort to men." This shows that prophecy is not just about future events; it's about bringing God's perspective into every moment of our lives. Prophetic insight helps us see the bigger picture and understand how God is working in our lives, even in the midst of challenges.

Through prophetic insight, we are given divine knowledge that empowers us to act wisely. Whether it's making decisions about our career, relationships, or ministry, prophetic insight provides the clarity we need to move forward with confidence.

Hearing the Voice of God

The foundation of prophetic insight is hearing the voice of God. This is a skill that requires practice and intimacy with the Holy Spirit. Many people struggle to discern God's voice because they are not tuned in to His frequency. Just like a radio that needs to be tuned to the right station, our spiritual ears must be attuned to the voice of God.

Jesus said in John 10:27, "My sheep hear My voice, and I know them, and they follow Me." This promise assures us that we are capable of hearing God's voice. However, it requires us to be intentional about spending time in His presence, listening for His direction, and quieting the noise of the world.

The more time we spend in prayer, worship, and reading the Word, the clearer God's voice becomes. Often, He speaks to us in a still, small voice, as He did with Elijah in 1 Kings 19:12. Other times, He may give us a strong impression, a vision, or even speak through a dream. Regardless of the method, God desires to communicate with us, and when we are sensitive to His voice, we open ourselves up to prophetic insight.

Living in the Prophetic

Living in the prophetic is not reserved for a select few; it is available to every believer who desires to walk closely with God. In fact, the Bible encourages us to "pursue love, and desire spiritual gifts, but especially that you may prophesy" (1 Corinthians 14:1).

This means that we should actively seek the gift of prophecy, not only for our own benefit but to edify others as well.

When you activate your day through prayer and worship, you position yourself to receive prophetic insight. You are essentially opening a direct line of communication with heaven, allowing God to reveal His plans and purposes for your life. As you become more attuned to His voice, you will begin to see things from a prophetic perspective.

This perspective transforms the way you view the world. You no longer react to circumstances based on fear or uncertainty. Instead, you approach life with divine insight, understanding that God is orchestrating everything for His glory. Whether you face trials, opportunities, or decisions, you are able to navigate them with wisdom and confidence because you have received prophetic insight.

The Life-changing Power of Prophetic Insight

Prophetic insight has the power to completely transform your life. When you receive revelation from God, you are equipped to live above the limitations of the natural world. No longer confined by what you can see or understand with your natural mind, you operate in the realm of the supernatural, where God's power is at work.

One of the key ways prophetic insight transforms your life is by giving you clarity in decision-making. Many times, we are faced with choices that seem difficult or overwhelming. Without God's guidance, we may make decisions based on our limited knowledge, only to realize later that we missed His plan. Prophetic insight eliminates this uncertainty by giving us access to God's perspective. We can move forward with confidence, knowing that we are following His will.

For example, in the Bible, we see how prophetic insight changed the course of people's lives. In 1 Samuel 16, God gave Samuel prophetic insight to anoint David as the next king of Israel, even though David was the youngest and least likely candidate by human standards. This prophetic revelation not only changed David's life but also the future of Israel.

In the same way, prophetic insight can open doors for you that you never thought possible. It may lead you to opportunities that seem unlikely or even impossible. But when God reveals His plan through prophetic insight, He makes a way for it to come to pass.

Another transformative aspect of prophetic insight is that it helps us avoid pitfalls and dangers. God often warns His people of impending danger through prophecy, giving them the opportunity to prepare or change course. In Acts 27, we see an example of this when Paul, through prophetic insight, warned the sailors not to continue their journey because of an impending storm. Though they ignored his warning, Paul's prophetic insight proved true, and eventually, he guided them to safety.

Prophetic insight also transforms our relationships. When we are tuned in to God's voice, He reveals things about the people around us, whether it's a word of encouragement, correction, or guidance. This enables us to speak life into their situations, to pray for them effectively, and to be instruments of God's love and grace.

Prophetic Insight for Everyday Life

It's important to understand that prophetic insight is not just for major life decisions or ministry purposes. God wants to give us prophetic revelation for every aspect of our lives, including the small, everyday things. Whether it's how to handle a difficult conversation at work, how to manage your finances, or even how to approach your health, God cares about every detail of your life and is willing to give you insight on how to navigate it.

Many believers think that the prophetic is only for church settings or spiritual matters. However, God is concerned about your whole life. He wants to give you insight into how to balance your family and work responsibilities, how to raise your children, and how to excel in your career. When you activate your day and invite God into every area of your life, you open yourself up to prophetic guidance that touches every aspect of your existence.

For example, you may be facing a financial challenge, unsure of how to make ends meet. Through prophetic insight, God may reveal a strategy for managing your resources more effectively or open up an unexpected opportunity for provision. Perhaps you're struggling in your relationships, unsure of how to resolve conflict. Prophetic insight can give you wisdom on how to approach the situation with grace and love, leading to healing and restoration.

God's prophetic insight is practical, applicable, and life-changing. It's not reserved for a specific time or place, it's available to you every day as you walk with Him.

Developing a Prophetic Lifestyle

Living in the prophetic requires more than just occasional moments of hearing from God. It's about cultivating a prophetic lifestyle where you are consistently tuned in to the voice of the Holy Spirit. This lifestyle is built on a foundation of prayer, worship, and obedience.

Prayer is the lifeline of the prophetic. It is through prayer that we engage with God, seek His face, and receive His revelations. A consistent prayer life keeps our spiritual ears sharp and our hearts sensitive to the Holy Spirit. As we pray, we position ourselves to hear God's voice clearly and accurately.

Worship is another key component of a prophetic lifestyle. Worship brings us into the presence of God, where we can experience His glory and power. When we worship, we shift our focus from ourselves to Him, creating an atmosphere where He can speak to us. Worship also aligns our hearts with God's, making it easier to discern His will.

Obedience is the final element of a prophetic lifestyle. When God speaks, we must be willing to obey. Prophetic insight is not just for information, it's for transformation. God reveals things to us so that we can act on them, bringing His kingdom to earth. As we obey His prophetic instructions, we see His power manifested in our lives.

Developing a prophetic lifestyle takes time, commitment, and intentionality. It's about walking closely with God, seeking His will in all things, and being willing to follow wherever He leads.

Prophetic insight is a gift that transforms our lives by giving us access to God's wisdom, direction, and revelation. When we activate our day through prayer, worship, and alignment with God's will, we open ourselves up to receive prophetic insight that empowers us to live victoriously.

The more we activate a prophetic lifestyle, the more attuned we become to God's voice, and the more we experience His transformative power in our everyday lives.

As you continue to activate your day, expect God to speak to you, guide you, and reveal His plans. Walk in prophetic power, and watch how your life is transformed as you align with His will and purpose.

CHAPTER 2

PATIENCE IN GOD'S PRESENCE

In a world that glorifies instant results and quick fixes, patience is often seen as an inconvenience or even a weakness. We are used to getting what we want when we want it, whether it's through fast food, instant messaging, or same-day delivery. But when it comes to our relationship with God, patience is not optional; it is essential. Waiting on God requires faith, trust, and, most importantly, patience. It is in these moments of waiting that we develop deeper intimacy with Him and experience His presence in ways that transform us.

The Call to Wait on God

Waiting on God is a recurring theme throughout the Bible. Time and time again, God's people are called to wait for His timing, His provision, and His answers. It's not because God is slow or unwilling to act, but because waiting is a vital part of the spiritual journey. Through waiting, we learn to depend on Him, to trust in His wisdom, and to surrender our timelines in exchange for His perfect will.

Psalm 27:14 says, "Wait on the Lord; be of good courage, and He shall strengthen your heart; wait, I say, on the Lord!" This verse highlights both the command and the promise attached to waiting on God. When we wait on Him, He strengthens our hearts. Patience becomes a place of spiritual growth, where God builds our character and deepens our faith.

But what does it mean to wait on God, particularly during prayer and worship? Waiting on God is not about sitting idly, hoping for something to happen. It is an active posture of faith where we engage with God through prayer, worship, and quietness of spirit. It is a time of seeking Him with expectation, knowing that He will respond in His time and in His way.

Why Patience is Essential in Prayer and Worship

Prayer and worship are two of the most intimate ways we connect with God. They are the avenues through which we pour out our hearts, express our love, and seek His face. However, these spiritual disciplines often require patience, especially when we don't receive immediate answers or feel an instant sense of God's presence.

In prayer, we may be tempted to rush through our requests, expecting God to respond as quickly as we ask. When the answer doesn't come right away, we might grow frustrated or even doubt whether God is listening. But prayer is not about getting quick answers; it's about developing a relationship with God. It's about trusting that He hears us and His timing is always perfect.

Similarly, we might expect to feel God's presence immediately or experience a powerful emotional response in worship. When that doesn't happen, we might think something is wrong with us or that God is distant. But worship is not about chasing feelings; it's about offering our hearts to God and waiting for Him to reveal Himself in His own time. Patience in prayer allows us to linger in His presence, press past distractions, and experience His glory's fullness.

Isaiah 40:31 reminds us of the reward that comes with patience in God's presence: "But those who wait on the Lord shall renew their strength; they shall mount up with wings like eagles, they shall run and not be weary, they shall walk and not faint." Waiting on God brings renewal, strength, and endurance. It allows us to soar above our circumstances and experience His sustaining grace.

The Challenge of Waiting

Waiting on God is not always easy, especially in a culture that values speed and efficiency. We are conditioned to expect immediate results; when they don't come, we can quickly become discouraged or impatient. But the waiting process is often where God does His most outstanding work in us.

One of the biggest challenges of waiting on God is the temptation to take matters into our own hands. We see this throughout Scripture. For example, Abraham and Sarah grew impatient waiting for the son God had promised them, and as a result, they tried to fulfill the promise through their means, leading to complications and heartache. Similarly, King Saul grew impatient waiting for the prophet Samuel and offered a sacrifice, resulting in God's rejection of him as king (1 Samuel 13:8-14).

These examples remind us of the importance of waiting on God's timing. When we rush ahead of God, we risk stepping outside of His will and missing His best for us. Patience in prayer and worship requires us to surrender our need for control and trust that God knows what He is doing, even when nothing is happening.

It's in the waiting that our faith is tested and strengthened. James 1:3-4 encourages us with these words: "knowing that the testing of your faith produces patience. But let patience have its perfect work, that you may be perfect and complete, lacking nothing." Through the process of waiting, God perfects us, making us complete and mature in our faith.

Learning to Linger in Worship

Worship is one of the most beautiful expressions of our love for God. It is a time when we offer ourselves to Him, acknowledging

His greatness and surrendering to His will. However, worship often requires us to linger, to remain in God's presence even when we don't feel anything right away.

Lingering in worship means that we don't rush through the experience. Instead, we allow ourselves to dwell in God's presence, waiting for Him to move. In a world that is constantly pulling us in different directions, learning to linger in worship is an act of surrender. It's a declaration that nothing is more important than spending time with God.

In 2 Chronicles 5:13-14, we see an example of the power of lingering in worship. During the dedication of Solomon's temple, the people of Israel gathered to worship God. They didn't rush through the songs or cut the service short. Instead, they worshipped with one voice, and the glory of the Lord filled the temple so powerfully that the priests could not continue ministering.

This is the kind of experience that comes when we are willing to linger in worship. God reveals His presence in ways that we could never imagine, and His glory transforms us. But this requires patience. It requires us to push past the distractions, the discomfort, and the urge to move on to the next thing.

Worship is not about getting through a set of songs or checking off a spiritual duty. It's about encountering the living God. And that encounter often comes in the waiting, in those moments when we quiet our hearts and focus solely on Him.

The Depth of Prayer in the Waiting

Just as worship calls us to linger in God's presence, prayer invites us into deep communion with Him, but this communion often unfolds over time. While we may come to God with specific requests or needs, prayer is more than just asking for things. It is about building a relationship, learning to hear His voice, and growing in intimacy with Him.

One of the most powerful examples of waiting on God in prayer comes from Jesus Himself. In the Garden of Gethsemane, on the night before His crucifixion, Jesus prayed fervently, seeking the Father's will. Luke 22:41-44 tells us that Jesus prayed so intensely that His sweat became like drops of blood. Yet, even in His anguish, Jesus waited on God's answer, ultimately surrendering His own will with the words, "Not My will, but Yours, be done."

Jesus' example shows us that prayer is not just about presenting our requests; it's about submitting to God's will, even when it's difficult. In those moments when we are waiting for an answer, we are not just waiting for God to fulfill our desires, we are waiting for our hearts to be aligned with His.

When we pray and don't receive an immediate response, it's easy to grow discouraged. We might wonder if God is listening or if He even cares. But the truth is, God is always listening, and He cares deeply. His silence is not a sign of disinterest but often a sign of His deeper work in our lives.

Psalm 37:7 encourages us to "Rest in the Lord, and wait patiently for Him." Resting in the Lord means trusting He is working behind the scenes, even when we can't see it. It means being still in His presence, knowing He is faithful to respond in His time.

Sometimes, the waiting is where the breakthrough happens. In those moments of silence, God is refining us, preparing us for what is to come. As we wait on Him in prayer, our faith is strengthened, our trust in Him deepens, and we are drawn closer to His heart.

The Reward of Patience in God's Presence

Waiting on God is never in vain. Those who wait on Him are always rewarded, not necessarily in the way they expect, but in the way that God knows is best. Isaiah 64:4 says, "For since the beginning of the world, men have not heard nor perceived by the ear, nor has the eye seen any God besides You, who acts for the one who waits for Him."

This verse reminds us that God acts for those who wait for Him. He is not passive; he works behind the scenes, orchestrates events, prepares hearts, and aligns circumstances according to His divine plan. Our job is to trust Him in the waiting and remain faithful in prayer and worship.

The reward of waiting on God is multifaceted. First, we experience a deepened relationship with Him. In the waiting, we learn to depend on Him more fully, and our intimacy grows. We also gain wisdom and discernment as we learn to hear His voice more clearly.

Second, we are strengthened for the journey ahead. Waiting on God equips us with the endurance we need to face the challenges of life. It builds spiritual resilience and prepares us for the battles we will face. As Isaiah 40:31 promises, those who wait on the Lord "shall renew their strength; they shall mount up with wings like eagles."

Finally, the waiting often leads to breakthrough. While we may not always see immediate results, God is faithful to answer our prayers in His time and in His way. The key is to trust that His timing is perfect and that His plans for us are good.

Testimonies of Patience Leading to Breakthroughs

Patience is one of the most challenging aspects of our walk with God, but it is also one of the most rewarding. Throughout the Bible and in modern-day testimonies, we see countless examples of how waiting on God leads to breakthroughs that exceed our expectations. These stories of patience remind us that God's timing is perfect and that He always works in ways that are far beyond what we can imagine.

The Story of Joseph: Patience in the Pit and Prison

One of the most powerful testimonies of patience in the Bible is the story of Joseph. His life is a clear demonstration of how God works through seasons of waiting, even when the circumstances seem unfair or hopeless.

Joseph was just a young man when he received prophetic dreams from God, showing him that he would one day rise to a position of great authority. However, the journey to that fulfillment was far from easy. Shortly after receiving these dreams, Joseph was betrayed by his own brothers, sold into slavery, and taken to Egypt. From there, his life seemed to go from bad to worse. He was falsely accused of a crime he didn't commit and thrown into prison.

For years, Joseph remained in prison, seemingly forgotten and left to wait. But during this time, God was working behind the scenes. Joseph's patience and faithfulness during this period of waiting allowed him to be positioned for a breakthrough that no one could have anticipated.

In Genesis 41, we see the culmination of Joseph's waiting. After years of being imprisoned and overlooked, Joseph was called upon by Pharaoh to interpret a dream that none of the wise men in Egypt could understand. Because of his prophetic insight, Joseph was not only freed from prison but elevated to second-in-command over all of Egypt. The very dreams that God had given Joseph years earlier came to pass in a way that exceeded anything he could have imagined.

Joseph's story teaches us that waiting on God is never wasted time. Even when it feels like we are stuck in a pit or a prison, God is working behind the scenes to orchestrate events that will lead to our breakthrough. Joseph's patience led to a divine appointment that changed not only his life but also the course of history for the nation of Israel.

The Israelites: Patience in the Wilderness

Another profound example of patience leading to breakthrough is found in the story of the Israelites and their journey through the wilderness. After being freed from slavery in Egypt, the Israelites were on their way to the Promised Land—a land flowing with milk and honey that God had prepared for them. However, what should have been a relatively short journey turned into 40 years of wandering in the wilderness.

During this time, the Israelites faced numerous challenges, including hunger, thirst, and attacks from enemies. Many of them grew impatient and even longed to return to Egypt, forgetting the suffering they had endured as slaves. Yet, despite their complaints and lack of faith at times, God remained faithful to His promise. He provided for them with manna from heaven, water from a rock, and protection from their enemies.

The period in the wilderness was not just a time of waiting—it was a time of preparation. God was teaching the Israelites to trust Him, to depend on Him for their daily needs, and to grow in their faith. When they finally entered the Promised Land under Joshua's leadership, they were equipped to take possession of the land because they had learned valuable lessons in the wilderness.

The Israelites' story reminds us that seasons of waiting are often seasons of preparation. Just as God used the wilderness to prepare the Israelites for their breakthrough, He uses our waiting periods to prepare us for the blessings He has in store. While it may be difficult to see in the moment, the wilderness is a place where God refines our character and strengthens our faith so that we are ready to receive His promises.

Hannah: Patience in Prayer

The story of Hannah is another beautiful testimony of patience leading to breakthroughs. Hannah was a woman who deeply desired to have a child, but she was unable to conceive for many years. This caused her great sorrow, especially because her husband's other wife, Peninnah, had children and often taunted Hannah for her barrenness.

Year after year, Hannah would go to the temple and pour out her heart to God in prayer, asking Him for a son. Despite her anguish, she remained faithful in her prayers, refusing to give up hope that God would answer her. In 1 Samuel 1:10-11, we see the depth of her desperation: "And she was in bitterness of soul, and prayed to the Lord and wept in anguish. Then she made a vow and said, 'O Lord of hosts, if You will indeed look on the affliction of Your maidservant and remember me, and not forget Your maidservant, but will give Your maidservant a male child, then I will give him to the Lord all the days of his life.'"

Hannah's persistence in prayer paid off. In time, God answered her prayers, and she gave birth to a son, Samuel, who would go on to become one of the greatest prophets in Israel's history. Hannah's breakthrough didn't just bring her personal joy, it had a profound impact on the entire nation of Israel, as Samuel played a crucial role in anointing Israel's first two kings, Saul and David.

Hannah's story is a testament to the power of patience in prayer. Even when it seems like our prayers are going unanswered, God hears us. He is faithful to respond in His perfect timing. Hannah's breakthrough came not only because of her prayers but also because of her willingness to wait on God and trust Him with the outcome. Her patience resulted in a blessing that went far beyond her personal desires, it shaped the future of a nation.

The Early Church: Patience in Persecution

The early church provides another example of patience leading to breakthrough, particularly in the face of persecution. After Jesus' ascension, the early Christians faced severe opposition from both the Roman authorities and the Jewish religious leaders. Many were imprisoned, beaten, and even martyred for their faith. Yet, despite the persecution, the early church remained patient and steadfast in their commitment to the gospel.

Acts 12 tells the story of Peter's miraculous escape from prison.

After King Herod had James, the brother of John, killed, Peter was arrested and put in prison, likely awaiting the same fate. However, instead of panicking, the early church responded with patience and prayer. Acts 12:5 says, "Peter was therefore kept in prison, but constant prayer was offered to God for him by the church."

In the middle of the night, an angel appeared to Peter, released him from his chains, and led him out of the prison without the guards noticing. Peter's release was a direct result of the church's patient prayers and faith in God's ability to deliver him.

This story illustrates how patience in the face of opposition can lead to miraculous breakthroughs. The early church could have easily given in to fear and despair, but instead, they trusted God and waited on Him to act. Their patience was rewarded with Peter's miraculous release and the continued growth of the church.

Persecution and opposition are often part of the Christian journey, but the early church teaches us that patience in these difficult seasons can lead to breakthroughs that glorify God and advance His kingdom.

Modern-Day Testimonies of Patience and Breakthrough

The principle of patience leading to breakthrough is not limited to biblical times. Even today, there are countless testimonies of people who have experienced incredible breakthroughs after patiently waiting on God.

Consider the story of a woman named Mary, who had been praying for the salvation of her husband for over 20 years. Despite her husband's hardened heart and resistance to the gospel, Mary continued to pray for him, believing that God would one day answer her prayers. During those years, she never stopped showing him the love of Christ, even when it seemed like he would never come to faith.

One day, seemingly out of the blue, her husband attended a

church service with her and gave his life to Christ. What seemed like an instant transformation was actually the result of decades of patient prayer and trust in God. Today, Mary's husband is a passionate follower of Jesus, and they serve together in their local church, leading others to Christ.

Mary's story is a powerful reminder that no prayer is wasted and that God's timing is perfect. Patience in prayer can lead to breakthroughs that not only transform individual lives but also impact entire families and communities.

Another modern-day testimony comes from a man named David, who had been out of work for over a year. Despite applying for countless jobs, he faced rejection after rejection. During this time, David wrestled with feelings of discouragement and frustration, wondering why God wasn't providing him with a job. But instead of giving up, David chose to remain patient, trusting that God had a plan.

One day, David received a job offer that was far beyond what he had expected. Not only was the position in his desired field, but it also offered a higher salary and better benefits than any of the jobs he had previously applied for. Looking back, David realized that God had been preparing him during his season of waiting, shaping his character and deepening his faith so that he would be ready for the opportunity when it came.

David's story is a reminder that God's delays are not denials. Sometimes, He allows us to wait because He is preparing something far better than we could have imagined. Patience in the waiting leads to breakthroughs that reveal His goodness and faithfulness.

The testimonies of Joseph, the Israelites, Hannah, the early church, and others have taught us that God is never late, we should instead wait on him.

CHAPTER 3

THE POWER OF GENEROSITY AND GIVING FORWARD

Generosity is more than just an act of kindness; it is a powerful spiritual principle that carries profound implications for our lives. The act of giving not only impacts those who receive but also transforms the giver in ways that are often immeasurable. When we understand the true nature of generosity, we begin to see it as an investment in our future, a way of participating in God's economy of abundance, and a pathway to experiencing His blessings.

Understanding the Principle of Giving

At its foundation, generosity is rooted in the character of God. He is the ultimate giver, and throughout Scripture, we see His generosity displayed in countless ways. From the creation of the world to the gift of His Son, God embodies the essence of giving. As His children, we are called to reflect His nature in our own lives.

The principle of giving is not just a financial matter; it encompasses every aspect of our lives. It includes giving our time, talents, and resources to bless others and advance God's kingdom. In 2 Corinthians 9:6-7, Paul writes, "But this I say: He who sows sparingly will also reap sparingly, and he who sows bountifully will also reap bountifully. So let each one give as he purposes in his heart, not grudgingly or of necessity; for God loves a cheerful giver." This passage reveals that the manner in which we give, our heart attitude, greatly influences the outcome.

When we give generously, we activate a divine principle that transcends natural understanding. It's a law of sowing and reaping that God established, and it applies not only to finances but to every area of our lives. What we put into the ground, whether it be kindness, love, or resources, will determine what we harvest in the future.

The Impact of Generosity on Our Future

Generosity has far-reaching effects that extend beyond the immediate moment of giving. It influences our future in several ways, and understanding these impacts can motivate us to develop a lifestyle of generosity.

Opening Doors of Opportunity

Generosity often opens doors that would otherwise remain closed. When we give freely, we create an atmosphere of trust and goodwill. This can lead to new opportunities, partnerships, and relationships that propel us forward. When we are generous with our time, for instance, we build connections with others, fostering collaboration and support that can lead to unexpected blessings.

In the Bible, we see numerous examples of individuals whose acts of generosity opened doors for them. Consider the story of the widow of Zarephath in 1 Kings 17. When the prophet Elijah approached her during a time of severe drought, she had only enough flour and oil to make a small meal for herself and her son before they would starve. However, she chose to share her last meal with Elijah. In return, God miraculously provided for her needs, ensuring that her flour and oil would not run out until the drought ended. Her act of generosity not only saved her life but also positioned her to receive God's miraculous provision.

Similarly, in our lives, acts of generosity can create opportunities that we never anticipated. By sowing seeds of kindness, we may find ourselves in situations where help and support flow back to us when we need it most.

Cultivating a Generous Heart

When we practice generosity, we cultivate a heart that is aligned with God's. Generosity transforms us from being self-centered to becoming others-focused. It shifts our perspective from scarcity to abundance, allowing us to see the needs of others and respond with compassion.

As we give, we begin to understand the true joy that comes from serving others. Acts of kindness and generosity create a cycle of positivity that enriches our lives and the lives of those around us. We become conduits of God's love, sharing His blessings with others.

In Acts 20:35, Paul reminds us of Jesus' words: "It is more blessed to give than to receive." This statement highlights the profound truth that true fulfillment comes from giving. When we live generously, we experience joy that far surpasses the temporary satisfaction of receiving.

Building a Legacy of Impact

Generosity allows us to leave a legacy that extends beyond our lifetime. When we invest in the lives of others, through financial support, mentorship, or acts of service, we create a ripple effect that can influence generations. Our acts of kindness can inspire others to do the same, creating a culture of generosity that transforms communities.

The Bible is filled with examples of individuals whose legacies were built on their generosity. For instance, Barnabas, a companion of Apostle Paul, was known for his generous spirit. He sold a piece of land and donated the proceeds to the early church, enabling the spread of the gospel. His legacy of generosity continues to inspire believers today.

In our own lives, we have the opportunity to build a legacy of impact through our generosity. When we invest in the lives of others, whether it's through charitable giving, supporting missions, or simply being present for those in need, we leave a mark that extends far beyond our time on earth.

Attracting Divine Favor

God honors those who are generous, and His favor often follows acts of giving. When we align ourselves with God's heart through generosity, we position ourselves to receive His blessings. Proverbs 11:25 states, "The generous soul will be made rich, and he who waters will also be watered himself." This verse encapsulates the principle that generosity leads to abundance.

God's favor can manifest in various ways, financial provision, opportunities, relationships, and peace. When we give generously, we can expect God to respond with His abundant blessings. This is not a formula for getting rich; rather, it is a promise of God's faithfulness to provide for those who reflect His character.

Strengthening Our Faith

Practicing generosity is also an act of faith. When we give, especially when it stretches us, we are demonstrating our trust in God's provision. We are saying, "I believe that God will meet my needs even when I give."

2 Corinthians 9:8 reminds us, "And God is able to make all grace abound toward you, that you, always having all sufficiency in all things, may have an abundance for every good work." This verse assures us that when we are generous, God ensures that we have everything we need to continue doing good works.

Every act of generosity strengthens our faith, helping us to rely more fully on God. The more we give, the more we experience His provision and faithfulness. This creates a cycle of trust where our faith grows stronger with each act of generosity.

The Spiritual Act of Giving Forward

Giving forward is a powerful extension of the principle of generosity. It is not just about giving to those in need; it is about investing in the future of others and advancing God's kingdom. The concept of giving forward means that we recognize the impact of our generosity not just in the present, but for the future.

Empowering Others to Thrive

When we give forward, we empower others to thrive. It is an investment in their potential and a commitment to their growth. This can take many forms, from providing scholarships to young people, supporting local businesses, or mentoring individuals in our communities.

Consider the story of the Good Samaritan in Luke 10:25-37. When the Samaritan came across a wounded traveler, he didn't just provide immediate assistance; he also ensured the man's future wellbeing by taking him to an inn and covering the costs of his care. This act of generosity went beyond a one-time gift; it was an investment in the man's recovery and future.

When we practice giving forward, we look for opportunities to make a lasting impact in the lives of others. We become advocates for those who may not have the means to thrive on their own. This mindset of empowerment transforms our communities and spreads hope and encouragement to those around us.

Creating a Culture of Generosity

Giving forward also contributes to creating a culture of generosity. When we model generosity in our lives, we inspire others to do the same. This ripple effect can change the atmosphere in our communities, leading to a more supportive and caring environment.

In Matthew 5:16, Jesus instructs us, "Let your light so shine before men, that they may see your good works and glorify your Father in heaven." Our acts of generosity serve as a reflection of God's love and grace, pointing others to Him. When we give forward, we shine the light of Christ, encouraging others to embrace a lifestyle of generosity.

A Legacy of Generosity

Giving forward is about leaving a legacy of generosity for future generations. When we invest in others and teach them the value of giving, we are instilling a mindset that can shape their lives and the lives of those they encounter.

Consider the impact of mentorship. When we take the time to invest in someone's life, we are not only affecting their present but also their future. Our generosity can inspire them to give forward as well, creating a cycle of generosity that extends far beyond ourselves.

The legacy of generosity has the power to change families, communities, and even nations. It is a gift that keeps on giving, and when we embrace the principle of giving forward, we participate in God's plan to bless others and advance His kingdom

How To Develop a Generous Heart

If we want to experience the full impact of generosity in our lives, we must cultivate a generous heart. Here are some practical steps to develop a spirit of generosity:

Start Small: Generosity doesn't have to begin with large gifts or significant acts; it often starts with small, meaningful gestures that can have a profound impact. Small acts of generosity can be as simple as offering a kind word to someone who seems down or giving a compliment to brighten someone's day. These little expressions of kindness can create ripples of positivity that encourage others to pay it forward.

In addition, consider lending a helping hand to a neighbor, whether it's assisting with groceries, offering to watch their kids for a while, or even helping with yard work. Such gestures promote community and strengthen relationships. Financial contributions don't always have to be large; even a small donation to a local charity or cause can make a difference. Many charities rely on the cumulative effect of many small gifts, which together can lead to significant support.

By starting small, we develop a mindset of giving that encourages us to look for opportunities to help others in our everyday lives. These simple actions not only benefit those around us but also enrich our own lives, promoting gratitude and fulfillment as we participate in a cycle of generosity.

Be Intentional: Being intentional about generosity involves actively seeking opportunities to bless others in our daily lives. This could manifest in various ways, such as volunteering time at local shelters, participating in community clean-up days, or mentoring someone who needs guidance. By making a conscious effort to engage in acts of kindness, we not only support those in need but also create a culture of generosity within our communities.

Consider setting aside time each week to volunteer for a cause that resonates with you. This could involve spending time at an animal shelter, participating in food drives, or helping at local schools. By committing to regular acts of service, we develop a habit of generosity that becomes part of our identity.

Also, being there for friends or family during tough times can make a significant impact. Offering to listen, share meals, or help with errands demonstrates our willingness to support those we care about. This intentionality in seeking out opportunities to give reinforces the notion that generosity is not merely an act but a lifestyle. When we prioritize giving, we create deeper connections with others and contribute to a more compassionate and supportive community.

Give Regularly: Making giving a regular part of your routine helps establish a mindset of generosity that aligns with your values and priorities. When we commit to giving consistently, it changes our approach to finances, time, and resources. This can start with tithing, where a portion of our income is set aside for our faith community or charitable organizations. By doing so, we not only support the work of our local church but also contribute to broader missions that help those in need around the world.

Regular giving can also take the form of monthly donations to charities that resonate with us. Whether it's supporting organizations focused on education, healthcare, or environmental conservation, establishing a habit of regular contributions ensures that we consistently invest in causes we believe in.

In addition, giving doesn't always have to be financial; it can also include regular volunteer work or donating goods. By incorporating acts of service into our routine, we create a culture of generosity within our lives and communities. This commitment to regular giving helps us remain grounded in our values, promotes gratitude, and allows us to witness the positive impact of our contributions over time, ultimately enriching our lives and the lives of others.

Pray for Opportunities: Ask God to open your eyes to opportunities for generosity. Pray for His guidance in how to use your resources to bless others. Be open to the leading of the Holy Spirit as He prompts you to give.

Embrace the Joy of Giving: Allow yourself to experience the joy that comes from giving. Celebrate the difference you are making in the lives of others, and let that joy motivate you to continue being generous.

Generosity is a powerful spiritual principle that has the potential to transform our lives and the lives of those around us. When we embrace a lifestyle of giving, we unlock blessings that go beyond material wealth. Generosity builds relationships, creates a legacy, and promote spiritual growth. It teaches us how to build a legacy for future generations.

Stories of Lives Transformed Through Generosity

Generosity has the power to change not only the lives of those who give but also those who receive. Throughout history and even in our daily lives, we encounter powerful testimonies of how acts of giving have led to life-altering transformations. These stories remind us that generosity is not just about meeting immediate needs; it's about sowing seeds that bring about lasting change.

The Widow's Mite: The Power of Small Acts of Generosity

One of the most perfect examples of generosity comes from the story of the widow's mite in Mark 12:41-44. As Jesus sat in the temple observing people give their offerings, many wealthy individuals gave large sums of money. Yet, it was the offering of a poor widow that caught His attention. She gave two small copper coins, worth only a fraction of a penny. In the world's eyes, her gift was insignificant, but Jesus saw the true value of her offering.

He said to His disciples, "Assuredly, I say to you that this poor widow has put in more than all those who have given to the treasury; for they all put in out of their abundance, but she out of her poverty put in all that she had, her whole livelihood" (Mark 12:43-44). The widow's act of generosity was not measured by the amount she gave, but by the heart behind it. She gave out of her lack, trusting God to provide for her.

This story has inspired countless individuals throughout history, showing that even the smallest acts of generosity can have a profound impact. The widow's faith and willingness to give all she had serve as a reminder that it's not about how much we give, but about the sacrifice and trust in God that accompanies our giving. Her story has transformed the hearts of many, encouraging them to give out of love and faith, regardless of their circumstances.

The Generosity of the Early Church: Transforming Communities

The early church provides a powerful example of how generosity can transform entire communities. In the book of Acts, we see a group of believers who were committed to living out their faith in tangible ways, including radical acts of generosity. Acts 2:44-45 describes their lifestyle: "Now all who believed were together, and had all things in common, and sold their possessions and goods, and divided them among all, as anyone had need."

This extraordinary level of generosity was not just about meeting physical needs; it was a reflection of the believers' unity and love for one another. Their willingness to share everything they had created a strong sense of community, where no one lacked anything. As a result, the early church grew rapidly, and the message of the gospel spread throughout the region.

One particular story from the early church stands out: the account of Barnabas, a man known for his generosity. In Acts 4:36-37, we read that Barnabas sold a piece of land and brought the money to the apostles, laying it at their feet to be distributed among those in need. His act of generosity not only met the immediate needs of the community but also set an example for others to follow.

Barnabas' generosity didn't stop with financial giving. He also played a crucial role in the life of apostle Paul. After Paul's conversion, many believers were skeptical of his intentions, given his past as a persecutor of the church. But Barnabas took Paul under his wing, vouching for him and introducing him to the apostles (Acts 9:26-27). Through his generosity of spirit and willingness to take a risk, Barnabas helped Paul become one of the most influential leaders in the early church.

The generosity of the early church and individuals like Barnabas transformed lives, not only by meeting material needs but also by fostering a spirit of unity, trust, and encouragement. Their example continues to inspire believers today to practice radical generosity and build communities that reflect the love of Christ.

The Impact of Anonymous Giving: A Story of Redemption

Sometimes, the most powerful acts of generosity come from those who give in secret, expecting nothing in return. One such story is the testimony of John, a man whose life was forever changed by an anonymous act of kindness.

John had grown up in a broken home and spent much of his youth in and out of trouble. By the time he reached adulthood, he was struggling with addiction and had lost all hope for a better future. One night, at his lowest point, he wandered into a church, desperate for help.

The church welcomed him with open arms, and over time, John began to attend services regularly. He felt drawn to the message of hope and redemption but was still burdened by his addiction and financial struggles. One Sunday, after a particularly moving service, John found an envelope in his coat pocket. Inside was a note that read, "God loves you and has a plan for your life. Use this to take the next step." Along with the note was a significant amount of money.

The anonymous gift allowed John to pay for a rehabilitation program that helped him break free from his addiction. More than the financial assistance, however, the act of kindness restored his faith in humanity and in God's love for him. John went on to rebuild his life, finding steady work and eventually becoming a leader in the church that had welcomed him.

The anonymous act of generosity didn't just change John's financial situation, it transformed his heart. It was a turning point in his life, showing him that he was valued and loved, even by people he didn't know. This story demonstrates how generosity, even when done in secret, can have a deep and lasting impact on someone's life.

The Ripple Effect of Generosity: A Businessman's Story

Generosity often creates a ripple effect, where one act of giving leads to multiple blessings and opportunities. This was the case for David, a successful businessman who experienced the transformative power of generosity in both his personal and professional life.

David had always been a generous man, regularly donating to his church and various charitable causes. However, one particular act of generosity stood out. A struggling single mother in his community was facing eviction due to financial difficulties. After hearing about her situation, David felt compelled to step in. Without hesitation, he paid her rent for several months, giving her the time she needed to get back on her feet.

What David didn't realize at the time was that this single act of generosity would have a profound impact on both the woman and his own life. The woman was able to keep her home, provide for her children, and eventually secure a stable job. But the story didn't end there.

Years later, David found himself in a difficult business situation. His company was on the verge of a major deal, but things weren't going as planned. Unexpectedly, one of the key decision-makers in the deal turned out to be the woman whose rent he had paid all those years ago. She had since become a successful executive, and she remembered David's generosity. Moved by his kindness, she advocated for his company, helping to secure the deal that would turn things around for his business.

David's story highlights the ripple effect of generosity. His act of kindness not only transformed the life of a struggling mother but also came full circle to bless him in his time of need. This story illustrates the principle that when we give freely, we often receive blessings in ways we could never have anticipated.

A Church's Generosity: Building Hope in a Community

Generosity can also transform entire communities, as seen in the story of a small church in a financially struggling neighborhood. The church had limited resources, but they were committed to making a difference in their community. Instead of focusing on what they didn't have, the members of the church began to look for ways to give, whether it was through volunteering their time, providing meals, or offering practical support to families in need.

One of their most significant projects was transforming an old, abandoned building into a community center where children could come after school for tutoring, mentorship, and a safe place to stay. The church members worked tirelessly to renovate the building, and although it required significant sacrifice, they were determined to complete the project.

As word spread about the church's efforts, local businesses and organizations began to take notice. Soon, donations of money, supplies, and volunteer hours poured in from all over the city. What started as a small act of generosity from a handful of church members grew into a citywide movement that transformed the entire neighborhood.

Today, the community center is a thriving hub of activity, providing support and hope to hundreds of children and families. The church's generosity not only improved the physical landscape of the neighborhood but also brought people together in a spirit of unity and love. This story shows how collective generosity can create lasting change, impacting generations to come.

These stories of generosity illustrate that giving has the power to transform lives in great and unexpected ways. Whether through small acts of kindness, radical communal sharing, or anonymous donations, generosity can open doors, restore hope, and create a ripple effect of blessings that extend far beyond the initial gift. As we continue to embrace the spiritual principle of giving, we not only impact the present but also shape the future for ourselves and those around us.

CHAPTER 4

MASTERING
SPIRITUAL DETAILS

In the prophetic realm, details matter. Spiritual growth and effectiveness in our walk with God depend significantly on how well we pay attention to the nuances of His voice, His leading, and His instructions. Just as in the natural world where success often hinges on attention to detail, the same holds true in the spiritual realm. God is a God of order and precision, and He expects His children to be alert and attentive to even the smallest things He reveals.

Mastering spiritual details is about tuning our hearts and minds to God's frequency, learning to discern His subtle promptings, and understanding that the smallest pieces of divine revelation can have profound implications. When we learn to focus on spiritual details, we gain clarity, avoid errors, and are positioned to fulfill God's purpose with precision and excellence.

The Role of Details in the Prophetic

Prophecy involves hearing from God and speaking forth His will. While many people think of prophecy as grand visions or significant revelations, much of the prophetic involves small, seemingly insignificant details that carry immense weight. Often, God will reveal just a fragment of His plan, a word, an image, or a scripture, and it is up to us to pay attention and seek further understanding.

In 1 Kings 19, we read the story of the prophet Elijah as he encountered God on Mount Horeb. After fleeing from Queen Jezebel, Elijah sought refuge in a cave, and there, God spoke to him. But God didn't speak through the powerful wind, the earthquake, or the fire. Instead, He spoke in "a still small voice" (1 Kings 19:12). Elijah's ability to hear and respond to that quiet whisper was critical in his next steps as a prophet. This story illustrates that the voice of God is often quiet and subtle, requiring a keen awareness and attention to detail to capture what He is saying.

In the prophetic, the details of what God reveals are often the keys to deeper understanding and accuracy. For instance, when interpreting dreams or visions, every element, from the colors to the symbols, to the people or objects present, holds significance. A detail as small as a specific word or phrase can change the entire meaning of a prophetic word. Therefore, mastering spiritual details is essential to ensure that the message is delivered accurately and effectively.

Examples of Spiritual Details in the Bible

Throughout the Bible, we see numerous examples where attention to detail in the prophetic realm was crucial to fulfilling God's purpose. The stories of the patriarchs, prophets, and apostles show that God often works through specific instructions, requiring His people to follow them with care.

One such example is found in the story of Noah. In Genesis 6, when God instructed Noah to build the ark, He didn't give vague or general instructions. Instead, He provided Noah with detailed measurements, materials, and specifications for constructing the ark. Genesis 6:14-16 records God's precise directions:

"Make yourself an ark of gopherwood; make rooms in the ark, and cover it inside and outside with pitch. And this is how you shall make it: The length of the ark shall be three hundred cubits, its width fifty cubits, and its height thirty cubits."

Noah's attention to these details was critical. If Noah had ignored or altered even one aspect of God's instructions, the ark may not have been able to withstand the floodwaters, and the entire mission could have been compromised. His faithfulness to follow God's detailed instructions led to the preservation of his family and the survival of humanity.

Another example is found in the life of Moses. When God gave Moses the plans for the tabernacle, He provided exact specifications for everything, from the dimensions of the structure to the materials used, to the design of the priestly garments. Exodus 25:9 says, "According to all that I show you, that is, the pattern of the tabernacle and the pattern of all its furnishings, just so you shall make it."

Moses' ability to pay attention to the smallest details ensured that the tabernacle would be a suitable dwelling place for God's presence. This attention to detail also honored God's holiness and sovereignty, demonstrating that His instructions were not to be taken lightly.

These biblical examples reveal that when God gives instructions, He expects us to follow them with precision. Spiritual details are not trivial; they are often the very things that determine whether or not we walk in alignment with God's will.

Why Details Matter in the Prophetic Realm

In the prophetic realm, details matter because they are often the difference between clarity and confusion, accuracy and misinterpretation. Here are several reasons why mastering spiritual details is essential in the prophetic:

Accuracy in Delivering Prophetic Words: A prophetic word can be powerful and life-changing, but it must be delivered accurately. Missing or misunderstanding a key detail can lead to confusion or even harm. When God reveals something prophetically, every aspect of the revelation is important. For instance, a single word or image may carry a symbolic meaning that, if overlooked, could change the entire message.

In 1 Corinthians 14:29, Paul instructs the church to "let two or three prophets speak, and let the others judge." This shows that prophecy should be weighed and examined carefully. Part of this examination involves paying attention to the details of the prophetic word. Is the word in alignment with Scripture? Are there nuances or specific elements that need further clarification? By mastering spiritual details, we ensure that the message is conveyed with integrity and accuracy.

Avoiding Presumption: In the prophetic realm, there is always the danger of presumption, assuming that we understand God's will based on our own ideas or experiences. However, prophetic revelation often contains layers of meaning that require careful attention and discernment. Presuming that we know what God is saying without taking the time to examine the details can lead to misinterpretation.

For example, in the book of Numbers, we read the story of Moses striking the rock to bring forth water for the Israelites. In Exodus 17, God instructed Moses to strike the rock at Horeb, and water would flow out for the people to drink. But in Numbers 20, when the people again complained of thirst, God gave Moses a different instruction: this time, he was to speak to the rock, not strike it. Moses, in his frustration, struck the rock again, disobeying God's detailed command. As a result, Moses was not allowed to enter the Promised Land.

This story highlights the importance of not assuming we know what God wants based on past experiences. Every instruction from God must be followed with attention to detail, as even a small deviation can lead to significant consequences.

Building Spiritual Discernment: Paying attention to spiritual details helps us grow in discernment. Discernment is the ability to distinguish between what is from God and what is not. By learning to recognize the subtle ways God speaks, we become more attuned to His voice and less susceptible to deception.

Hebrews 5:14 speaks of those "who by reason of use have their senses exercised to discern both good and evil." This discernment comes through practice and experience, particularly in the prophetic realm. The more we pay attention to the details of how God speaks, the more refined our spiritual senses become. Over time, we learn to distinguish between God's voice, our own thoughts, and the enemy's distractions.

Receiving Full Revelation: Sometimes, God reveals His will in stages, giving us small pieces of the puzzle rather than the full picture all at once. If we dismiss the small details, we may miss out on the fullness of what God wants to reveal. In the prophetic, God often begins with a single word, image, or impression. As we act on that initial revelation and seek Him for more, He begins to unfold His plan in greater detail.

In the book of Daniel, we see an example of this process. Daniel received a series of visions and dreams that were filled with complex details. Rather than assuming he understood everything, Daniel sought God for clarity and interpretation. In Daniel 7:16, he says, "I came near to one of those who stood by, and asked him the truth of all this. So he told me and made known to me the interpretation of these things." Daniel's willingness to seek understanding of the details allowed him to receive deeper revelation.

Similarly, in our own lives, God may give us small pieces of revelation that require patience and persistence to fully understand. Mastering spiritual details involves taking the time to seek God for further insight, trusting that He will reveal more as we walk in obedience.

Honoring God's Precision: Ultimately, paying attention to spiritual details is about honoring the God of precision.

Throughout Scripture, we see that God is not haphazard in His actions. From the design of the universe to the specific instructions He gave His people, God operates with intentionality and precision. When we approach the prophetic with the same level of care, we demonstrate our reverence for His ways.

Proverbs 3:5-6 reminds us to "trust in the Lord with all your heart, and lean not on your own understanding; in all your ways acknowledge Him, and He shall direct your paths." By acknowledging God in the details, we position ourselves to receive His direction and walk in alignment with His will.

Practical Steps to Mastering Spiritual Details

Mastering spiritual details requires intentionality and discipline. Here are some practical steps to help you grow in this area:

Develop a Consistent Prayer Life: Prayer is the foundation for hearing from God and discerning His voice. Make time each day to seek God in prayer, asking Him to open your spiritual ears and eyes to the details He wants to reveal.

Study the Word of God: The Bible is filled with examples of God's precision and attention to detail. As you study Scripture, ask the Holy Spirit to reveal the deeper meanings behind specific words, phrases, and instructions. This will sharpen your ability to recognize spiritual details in your own life.

Practice Listening for God's Voice: Set aside time to practice listening for God's voice. Begin by asking Him a specific question and waiting for His response. As you listen, pay attention to the small impressions, images, or thoughts that come to mind. Write them down, even if they seem insignificant, and ask God for further clarity.

Journal Your Prophetic Impressions: Keeping a journal of prophetic impressions, dreams, and visions can help you track the details of what God is revealing over time. Review your journal regularly to see patterns or connections that may not have been apparent at first.

Seek Wise Counsel: When you receive prophetic words or impressions, seek counsel from trusted spiritual mentors or leaders. They can help you discern the details and provide guidance on how to respond.

Be Patient and Persistent: God often reveals His will in stages. Don't rush the process. Be patient, and continue seeking Him for further understanding. Trust that He will reveal the necessary details in His timing.

Testimonies of God Using Small Details for Big Breakthroughs

The Bible and personal testimonies are filled with examples of how small details in the prophetic realm have led to significant breakthroughs. These stories demonstrate that God is always working in the minutiae, orchestrating events in ways that we may not initially recognize. Yet, when we pay attention to these divine details, they become the keys that unlock major victories, miracles, and answers to prayer.

David and the Sling: A Small Weapon for a Giant Breakthrough

Perhaps one of the most famous examples of God using a small detail for a massive breakthrough is the story of David and Goliath. When David, a young shepherd boy, faced Goliath, a seasoned warrior, no one believed that David stood a chance. Goliath was fully armed with heavy armor and weapons, while David appeared defenseless with only a sling and five smooth stones.

The detail of David choosing five smooth stones from the brook may seem insignificant at first glance, but it was a critical element in the victory God had planned. David's decision to rely on something as simple as a sling, rather than the traditional armor or weapons offered to him by King Saul, was a reflection of his faith in God. He understood that the battle was not about physical strength or military strategy but about trusting in the power of God.

In 1 Samuel 17:45, David boldly declares, "You come to me with a sword, with a spear, and with a javelin. But I come to you in the name of the Lord of hosts, the God of the armies of Israel, whom you have defied." Armed with only a sling, David hurled one of the small stones, striking Goliath on the forehead, and the giant fell. This seemingly small act, which is the detail of choosing the right weapon, resulted in a massive breakthrough not only for David but for the entire nation of Israel.

The story of David and Goliath reminds us that God often works through small, seemingly insignificant details to bring about major victories. David's choice to use the sling was more than a tactical decision; it was a prophetic act of faith, showing that God can use anything, no matter how small, to accomplish His purpose.

Elijah and the Cloud: A Small Sign of a Mighty Storm

Another powerful testimony of God using a small detail for a big breakthrough is found in the story of the prophet Elijah and the drought in Israel. For three years, there had been no rain in the land, and the people were desperate. After confronting the false prophets of Baal and seeing God's power displayed in fire on Mount Carmel, Elijah prayed for rain to end the drought.

In 1 Kings 18:41-45, we read that Elijah prayed fervently for rain, but at first, there was no sign of it. Elijah sent his servant to look toward the sea seven times before the servant finally reported seeing "a cloud, as small as a man's hand, rising out of the sea" (1 Kings 18:44). This tiny cloud might have seemed insignificant, but to Elijah, it was the prophetic detail he had been waiting for.

Elijah immediately recognized that this small cloud was a sign of the breakthrough God was about to bring. He instructed his servant to prepare for the coming storm, and shortly afterward, the sky grew black with clouds, and a heavy rain began to fall, ending the drought.

This story teaches us that small prophetic details can be indicators of much larger things to come. What appeared to be a tiny, insignificant cloud was actually the first sign of a mighty outpouring of rain that would transform the entire land. Elijah's attentiveness to this small detail allowed him to act in faith and prepare for the breakthrough that God was bringing.

Naaman's Healing: A Small Act of Obedience with Big Results

In 2 Kings 5, we find the story of Naaman, a commander in the army of Syria who suffered from leprosy. Naaman had heard of the prophet Elisha's ability to heal, and he traveled to Israel in hopes of being cured. When he arrived, Elisha sent a messenger to instruct Naaman to wash himself seven times in the Jordan River to be healed.

Naaman was initially offended by this instruction. He expected Elisha to perform some grand, dramatic healing ritual, and the idea of washing in the dirty waters of the Jordan seemed beneath him. In 2 Kings 5:11-12, Naaman expresses his frustration, saying, "I thought he would surely come out to me and stand and call on the name of the Lord his God, wave his hand over the spot, and cure me of my leprosy. Are not Abana and Pharpar, the rivers of Damascus, better than all the waters of Israel?"

However, Naaman's servants persuaded him to obey the prophet's simple instruction, and when he finally humbled himself and dipped in the Jordan seven times, his leprosy was completely healed. What seemed like a small, trivial act, washing in a river, became the key to Naaman's miraculous healing.

This story highlights the importance of obedience to the small details in God's instructions. Naaman's healing didn't come through grand gestures or dramatic rituals; it came through his willingness to obey a simple command. This shows us that even the smallest acts of obedience can lead to life-changing breakthroughs when they are done in faith and humility.

The Widow's Oil: A Small Jar Leading to Overflow

In 2 Kings 4:1-7, we read about a widow who was in desperate need. Her husband had died, leaving her with a large debt that she couldn't repay. As a result, her creditor was threatening to take her two sons as slaves. In her distress, she went to the prophet Elisha for help.

Elisha asked her, "What do you have in the house?" The widow responded that she had nothing except a small jar of oil. This small detail, a seemingly insignificant jar of oil, became the key to her breakthrough.

Elisha instructed her to borrow empty vessels from her neighbors, as many as she could find, and then to pour the oil from her small jar into the empty vessels. As she poured, the oil miraculously kept flowing until all the vessels were filled. Elisha then told her to sell the oil, pay off her debts, and live on the rest.

This story demonstrates how God can take something small, like a jar of oil, and multiply it into abundance. The widow's obedience to the prophetic instruction, even though it didn't make sense in the natural, resulted in a miraculous provision that saved her family. What started as a small act of faith, pouring oil into empty vessels, led to a major breakthrough of financial freedom.

Jesus' Parable of the Mustard Seed: Small Faith for Big Results

Jesus often taught about the power of small things in the Kingdom of God. One of His most well-known parables is the parable of the mustard seed, found in Matthew 17:20 and Luke 17:6. Jesus said that if we have faith as small as a mustard seed, we can move mountains. Though the mustard seed is one of the smallest seeds, it grows into one of the largest plants, providing shelter and sustenance for many.

This parable illustrates that even the smallest amount of faith, when placed in God's hands, can lead to extraordinary results. The key is not the size of our faith but the power of the One in whom we place our faith. Jesus wanted His disciples to understand that God honors faith, no matter how small it may seem, and that He can use it to bring about monumental breakthroughs.

The mustard seed parable continues to inspire believers today to act in faith, even when they feel their faith is weak or insignificant. God doesn't require grand gestures of faith, He honors the smallest steps of trust and obedience.

Esther: A Small Act of Courage Saving a Nation

The story of Queen Esther is another powerful testimony of how small details can lead to significant breakthroughs. Esther, a Jewish woman who became queen of Persia, found herself in a position where she could either remain silent or risk her life to save her people. Haman, a high-ranking official in the king's court, had plotted to annihilate the Jewish people, and Esther's cousin Mordecai urged her to speak up on behalf of her people.

Esther was initially hesitant, knowing that approaching the king without being summoned could result in her death. However, Mordecai's words encouraged her: "Who knows whether you have come to the kingdom for such a time as this?" (Esther 4:14).

Esther's decision to act in this small, specific moment was a turning point. She called for a three-day fast among the Jewish people and then approached the king with her request. Her small act of courage, speaking up at the right time, ultimately saved the entire Jewish nation from destruction.

This story shows that sometimes, the details of timing and courage can make all the difference in a breakthrough. Esther's willingness to act in a small but critical moment led to a massive victory for her people. It reminds us that God often orchestrates the timing of our actions and that even small, seemingly insignificant decisions can have a lasting impact.

The Feeding of the 5,000: A Small Meal Feeding Thousands

One of the most famous miracles of Jesus is the feeding of the 5,000, recorded in all four Gospels. In this story, Jesus is teaching a large crowd, and as the day grows late, the disciples realize that the people have nothing to eat. They urge Jesus to send the crowd away so they can find food, but Jesus has a different plan.

A young boy in the crowd offers his small lunch, five loaves of bread and two fish. It seems like an insignificant offering in the face of such a large need, but Jesus takes the small meal, blesses it, and begins distributing it to the crowd. Miraculously, the food multiplies, and everyone is fed with plenty left over.

This story demonstrates that no gift is too small for God to use. The boy's simple offering became the catalyst for a miracle that fed thousands. What seemed like an insignificant detail, that is, a small lunch, became the key to one of the most extraordinary miracles in Jesus' ministry.

These testimonies illustrate that God often uses the small details, whether it's a stone, a cloud, a jar of oil, or a small act of courage, to bring about major breakthroughs. When we pay attention to the details and trust God's instructions, even when they seem insignificant, we position ourselves to experience His power in extraordinary ways.

CHAPTER 5

LIMITLESS POSSIBILITIES THROUGH GOD'S COMPOUND INTEREST

I n the natural world, the concept of compound interest is a powerful force. When you invest a sum of money and allow the interest to compound over time, it grows exponentially. The longer you leave the investment, the more it multiplies, and what started as a small amount can eventually become a significant sum. This same principle can be applied to the spiritual realm. God's "compound interest" operates on the principle that when we invest in His kingdom, through prayer, faith, obedience, generosity, and service, He multiplies our efforts in ways that far exceed what we could accomplish on our own. Spiritual compound interest represents the exponential growth of our spiritual investments, and through it, God opens the door to limitless possibilities.

What is Spiritual Compound Interest?

Spiritual compound interest refers to the cumulative effect of our faithfulness, obedience, and dedication to God's purposes over time. Just as in the financial world, where compounding causes interest to grow faster as time progresses, so in the spiritual realm, small acts of faith and obedience have a multiplying effect as we continue to walk in alignment with God's will. The key difference is that, while financial compound interest operates within the natural realm, spiritual compound interest is backed by the supernatural power of God, which makes the growth we experience limitless.

To understand spiritual compound interest, we must first recognize that every step of obedience, every prayer, every act of kindness, and every seed we sow into the kingdom of God is like an investment. We may not always see immediate results, but as we continue to trust God and remain faithful, these investments begin to multiply in ways we never imagined. Over time, the spiritual growth we experience and the impact we have on others begin to compound, leading to exponential growth in our lives and in the kingdom of God.

The principle of spiritual compound interest is deeply rooted in Scripture. Throughout the Bible, we see God's promise of multiplication, both in the natural and the spiritual realm. One of the most well-known examples of this is found in the parable of the talents in Matthew 25:14-30. In this parable, Jesus tells the story of a master who entrusted his servants with different amounts of money (referred to as talents) before going on a journey. Two of the servants invested their talents wisely, and when the master returned, they were able to present him with a multiplied return on their investment. The master rewarded these servants for their faithfulness, saying, "Well done, good and faithful servant; you have been faithful over a few things, I will make you ruler over many things. Enter into the joy of your lord" (Matthew 25:23).

The third servant, however, buried his talent in the ground, fearing that he would lose it. When the master returned, the servant presented him with the exact amount he had been given, with no growth or multiplication. The master rebuked this servant for his lack of faith and action, taking the talent away from him and giving it to the servant who had multiplied his investment.

This parable illustrates the principle of spiritual compound interest. God entrusts us with resources, whether they be talents, time, finances, or spiritual gifts, and He expects us to invest them wisely. When we do so, He multiplies our efforts and rewards us with even greater opportunities to serve Him and impact the world around us.

Another example of this principle is found in Galatians 6:7-9, where Paul writes, "Do not be deceived, God is not mocked; for whatever a man sows, that he will also reap. For he who sows to his flesh will of the flesh reap corruption, but he who sows to the Spirit will of the Spirit reap everlasting life. And let us not grow weary while doing good, for in due season we shall reap if we do not lose heart."

This passage highlights the importance of perseverance in spiritual investments. Just as in the financial world, where compound interest takes time to accumulate, spiritual compound interest requires patience and faithfulness. We may not always see the results of our efforts right away, but if we continue to sow to the Spirit, through prayer, obedience, and service, we will eventually experience a harvest that is far greater than anything we could have imagined.

The Power of Small Investments

One of the most encouraging aspects of spiritual compound interest is that it doesn't require us to make grand gestures or enormous sacrifices in order to experience exponential growth. Just as a small financial investment can grow over time through the power of compounding, so too can small spiritual investments multiply as we continue to walk in faith.

Jesus illustrated this principle in the parable of the mustard seed in Matthew 13:31-32. He said, "The kingdom of heaven is like a mustard seed, which a man took and sowed in his field. Indeed, it is the least of all the seeds; but when it is grown, it is greater than the herbs and becomes a tree, so that the birds of the air come and nest in its branches." The mustard seed is one of the smallest seeds, yet when it is planted, it grows into a large tree that provides shelter and sustenance for many. This parable shows that even the smallest acts of faith, when sown in God's kingdom, have the potential to produce exponential growth.

Another example of small investments leading to great results is the story of the widow's offering in Mark 12:41-44. As Jesus sat in the temple watching people bring their offerings, many wealthy individuals gave large sums of money. However, it was the small offering of a poor widow, just two small copper coins, that caught Jesus' attention. He told His disciples, "Assuredly, I say to you that this poor widow has put in more than all those who have given to the treasury; for they all put in out of their abundance, but she out of her poverty put in all that she had, her whole livelihood."

Though the widow's offering was small in the eyes of the world, Jesus recognized the significance of her sacrifice. Her act of generosity, though seemingly insignificant, was an investment that would yield spiritual dividends far greater than the large offerings of the wealthy. This story reminds us that God values the heart behind our investments more than the size of the investment itself. When we give, serve, or pray with a sincere heart, even the smallest acts can lead to profound results in God's kingdom.

Exponential Growth through Faith and Obedience

One of the most exciting aspects of spiritual compound interest is the potential for exponential growth. When we invest in God's kingdom, whether through prayer, generosity, or acts of service, God doesn't simply add to our efforts; He multiplies them. This exponential growth is often beyond what we can measure or comprehend, as God's ways are higher than our ways (Isaiah 55:8-9).

A powerful example of exponential growth through faith and obedience is the story of the feeding of the 5,000 in Matthew 14:13-21. In this story, a large crowd had gathered to hear Jesus teach, but as the day wore on, the people became hungry. The disciples urged Jesus to send the crowd away to find food, but Jesus had a different plan. A young boy offered his small lunch, five loaves of bread and two fish, which seemed woefully inadequate to feed thousands of people. Yet, Jesus took the small offering, blessed it, and multiplied it until there was more than enough to feed everyone, with twelve baskets of leftovers remaining.

This miracle demonstrates the power of exponential growth when we place our faith in God. The boy's small offering, when placed in Jesus' hands, became the key to a miraculous multiplication that fed thousands. What seemed insignificant in the natural became the catalyst for a supernatural breakthrough. This story reminds us that when we offer God what we have, no matter how small, He is able to multiply it beyond our wildest expectations.

Similarly, in John 15:5, Jesus tells His disciples, "I am the vine, you are the branches. He who abides in Me, and I in him, bears much fruit; for without Me you can do nothing." The key to experiencing exponential growth in the spiritual realm is abiding in Christ, remaining connected to Him through faith, prayer, and obedience. When we abide in Him, our efforts are no longer limited by our own abilities. Instead, we tap into the limitless power of God, and the fruit we bear becomes abundant and enduring.

The Law of Multiplication in God's Kingdom

The law of multiplication is a recurring theme throughout Scripture, and it is closely tied to the principle of spiritual compound interest. God's desire is not just to add to our lives, but to multiply His blessings, His favor, and His impact through us. This multiplication happens when we invest in His kingdom with faith and obedience, trusting that He will take our small efforts and use them for His glory.

One of the most striking examples of multiplication in the Bible is found in Genesis 22:17, where God makes a covenant with Abraham, saying, "Blessing I will bless you, and multiplying I will multiply your descendants as the stars of the heaven and as the sand which is on the seashore; and your descendants shall possess the gate of their enemies." God's promise to Abraham was not just about having many children; it was a promise of exponential growth and influence that would extend far beyond Abraham's lifetime. Today, we see the fulfillment of this promise in the countless descendants of Abraham, both physically and spiritually, who continue to impact the world.

The same law of multiplication applies to us as believers. When we invest in God's kingdom, whether through prayer, generosity, or acts of service, He multiplies our efforts in ways that ripple through eternity. The small seeds we sow today can lead to a harvest of blessings, opportunities, and impact that far exceed what we could accomplish on our own.

In Luke 6:38, Jesus says, "Give, and it will be given to you: good measure, pressed down, shaken together, and running over will be put into your bosom. For with the same measure that you use, it will be measured back to you." This promise of multiplication applies not only to our financial giving but to every area of our lives. When we give generously, serve faithfully, and invest in God's kingdom with a heart of obedience, we open the door to limitless possibilities and exponential growth.

Living with an Eternal Perspective

One of the keys to understanding and embracing spiritual compound interest is living with an eternal perspective. In the financial world, compound interest works best when we allow our investments to grow over time, without constantly withdrawing or spending the returns. The same is true in the spiritual realm. When we invest in God's kingdom with a long-term perspective, trusting that our efforts will yield eternal rewards, we position ourselves for exponential growth that goes far beyond our earthly life.

In Matthew 6:19-21, Jesus encourages us to live with an eternal perspective, saying, "Do not lay up for yourselves treasures on earth, where moth and rust destroy and where thieves break in and steal; but lay up for yourselves treasures in heaven, where neither moth nor rust destroys and where thieves do not break in and steal. For where your treasure is, there your heart will be also."

This scripture reminds us that our spiritual investments have eternal significance. The prayers we pray, the seeds we sow, and the acts of service we perform may not always yield immediate results in the natural realm, but they are storing up treasures in heaven that will last for eternity. When we live with this eternal perspective, we are more willing to invest in God's kingdom, knowing that the return on our investment will far outweigh anything we could gain in this life.

Practical Ways to Invest in God's Kingdom

If we want to experience the power of spiritual compound interest and exponential growth, we must be intentional about making regular investments in God's kingdom. Below are some practical ways to invest spiritually:

Prayer: Prayer is one of the most powerful ways to invest in God's kingdom. Each time we pray, we are sowing seeds of faith that will yield a harvest in God's perfect timing. Make a commitment to pray regularly for God's will to be done in your life, your family, and your community.

Generosity: Whether it's giving financially, sharing your time, or offering your talents, generosity is a powerful investment that God multiplies. Look for opportunities to give, whether it's to your local church, a charitable organization, or someone in need.

Service: Acts of service, whether big or small, are investments in God's kingdom. Whether it's volunteering at your church, mentoring someone, or simply helping a neighbor, every act of service is a seed that God can multiply.

Faithfulness: Faithfulness in the small things is key to experiencing spiritual compound interest. Whether it's being consistent in your daily devotions, showing up faithfully at your job, or serving in your local church, God honors faithfulness and uses it to bring about exponential growth.

When we understand the principle of spiritual compound interest, we begin to see the limitless possibilities that God has for our lives. Small investments, whether in prayer, generosity, or service, lead to exponential growth as we remain faithful to God's calling. By living with an eternal perspective and trusting in God's power to multiply our efforts, we unlock a life of abundance, fruitfulness, and impact that reaches far beyond what we could achieve on our own.

As you continue to invest in God's kingdom, trust that He is working behind the scenes, multiplying your efforts and preparing a harvest that will far exceed your expectations. The seeds you sow today will yield a bountiful harvest tomorrow, and through the power of God's spiritual compound interest, you will experience the limitless possibilities that come from walking in alignment with His will.

Testimonies of God's Limitless Possibilities

When we trust in God's compound interest, that is, His ability to multiply our small investments of faith, prayer, and obedience, the results can be astounding. Throughout history, both in biblical accounts and modern-day testimonies, we see powerful examples of God's limitless possibilities at work. These stories remind us that no situation is too hopeless, no dream is too big, and no resource is too small for God to use and transform into something extraordinary.

By understanding that God is not bound by the limitations we face, we open ourselves up to His divine multiplication and supernatural breakthroughs. Let's look at some testimonies that showcase the remarkable ways God has taken what appeared to be small or impossible situations and turned them into something far beyond human comprehension.

Abraham and Sarah: The Promise of a Limitless Legacy

One of the most well-known biblical testimonies of God's limitless possibilities is the story of Abraham and Sarah. God promised Abraham that He would make him the father of many nations and that his descendants would be as numerous as the stars in the sky. However, Abraham and Sarah were childless, and as they advanced in age, it seemed impossible that God's promise would be fulfilled.

In Genesis 17:16, God reaffirmed His promise to Abraham, telling him that Sarah would bear a son, despite her old age. "I will bless her and also give you a son by her; then I will bless her, and she shall be a mother of nations; kings of peoples shall be from her." This promise must have seemed absurd to them at the time. Sarah was 90 years old, well past the age of childbearing, and Abraham was 100. Yet God is not limited by the natural constraints of time, age, or physical ability.

Sarah laughed at the thought of having a child at her age, but God's response was clear: "Is anything too hard for the Lord?" (Genesis 18:14). This rhetorical question underscores the reality that there are no limits to what God can do. Despite their doubts, Sarah did conceive and bore a son, Isaac, through whom God's covenant promises to Abraham were fulfilled.

Abraham and Sarah's story is a testament to God's faithfulness and His ability to bring about the impossible. Even in situations where human logic says "no," God says "yes." Their testimony serves as a reminder that, when we place our trust in God, He can bring to fruition the most improbable promises and create a legacy that impacts generations.

The Multiplication of the Widow's Oil: An Overflowing Supply

The story of the widow's oil, found in 2 Kings 4:1-7, provides another powerful testimony of God's limitless possibilities through multiplication. The widow was in desperate need, her husband had died, leaving her with significant debt, and her two sons were about to be taken as slaves to pay off the creditor. With nothing left except a small jar of oil, she turned to the prophet Elisha for help.

Elisha gave her an instruction that seemed impossible: "Go, borrow vessels from everywhere, from all your neighbors—empty vessels; do not gather just a few" (2 Kings 4:3). He then told her to pour out her oil into these vessels. As she followed his instructions, the small jar of oil miraculously filled every vessel she had collected. When the last vessel was filled, the oil stopped flowing. Elisha then told her to sell the oil, pay off her debts, and live on the remaining proceeds.

What began as a small amount of oil, seemingly insignificant, became a limitless supply that provided for the widow and her family. This story demonstrates that God can take even the smallest resource and multiply it beyond measure. The widow's testimony shows us that, in God's hands, what we think is inadequate or insufficient can become more than enough. It's a reminder that God's resources are limitless, and when we trust Him, He provides in ways that defy human understanding.

The Israelites in the Wilderness: Provision from Heaven

The story of the Israelites in the wilderness is a powerful example of God's limitless possibilities when it comes to provision. After being delivered from slavery in Egypt, the Israelites found themselves wandering in the wilderness for forty years, facing hunger, thirst, and the harsh conditions of the desert. They had no natural means of survival, yet God provided for them in supernatural ways that went beyond what anyone could have imagined.

In Exodus 16, we read about how God sent manna from heaven to feed the Israelites. Each morning, the manna would appear on the ground like dew, and the people would gather it to eat. This miraculous provision continued every day for forty years until they reached the Promised Land. In addition to the manna, God provided water from a rock and quail for meat when they complained of hunger.

God's provision in the wilderness was a daily reminder to the Israelites of His limitless power and care. Despite their lack of resources and their constant grumbling, God continued to meet their needs in ways that transcended natural laws. The testimony of the Israelites shows us that, no matter how dire our circumstances may seem, God is always able to provide for us. His provision is not limited by our environment, our resources, or our ability to understand how it will happen.

This story also emphasized the importance of trusting God day by day. The Israelites were instructed to gather only enough manna for each day, teaching them to rely on God's daily provision rather than trying to store up more than they needed. This principle of daily trust is key to experiencing God's limitless possibilities. When we trust Him to provide for us one step at a time, we open the door for Him to work in ways that go beyond what we can see or anticipate.

The Raising of Lazarus: Life Out of Death

One of the most striking examples of God's limitless possibilities is found in the story of Lazarus, as recorded in John 11. Lazarus, a close friend of Jesus, had fallen seriously ill, and his sisters, Mary and Martha, sent word to Jesus, asking Him to come and heal their brother. However, by the time Jesus arrived in Bethany, Lazarus had already been dead for four days. Humanly speaking, it was too late, Lazarus was beyond help, and his body had begun to decay.

Martha expressed her grief and disappointment to Jesus, saying, "Lord, if You had been here, my brother would not have died" (John 11:21). But Jesus responded with a powerful declaration: "I am the resurrection and the life. He who believes in Me, though he may die, he shall live" (John 11:25). Despite the seemingly hopeless situation, Jesus knew that death was not a limitation for God.

Jesus then went to the tomb, commanded the stone to be rolled away, and called out, "Lazarus, come forth!" (John 11:43). To everyone's astonishment, Lazarus emerged from the tomb, fully alive and restored.

The raising of Lazarus is a profound testimony of God's power over life and death. What seemed like an irreversible situation, death itself, was no obstacle for Jesus. This miracle demonstrates that God's possibilities are truly limitless. Even when all hope seems lost, God is able to bring life out of death, healing out of brokenness, and restoration out of despair. Lazarus' resurrection reminds us that no situation is too far gone for God to redeem and transform.

The Story of Jabez: A Prayer for Increase

The brief but powerful story of Jabez in 1 Chronicles 4:9-10 offers a testimony of God's ability to bring limitless possibilities into the life of someone who seeks Him in faith. Jabez is described as being more honorable than his brothers, yet his name, which means "pain," reflected the difficult circumstances of his birth. Despite this, Jabez prayed a bold prayer, asking God for blessing and increase: "Oh, that You would bless me indeed, and enlarge my territory, that Your hand would be with me, and that You would keep me from evil, that I may not cause pain!"

Jabez's prayer is significant because it shows that he believed in the limitless possibilities of God's favor and blessing. He asked for more; more influence, more territory, more of God's hand upon his life, and God granted his request. Though Jabez's story is brief, it demonstrates that God is not limited by our past, our circumstances, or even our name. When we come to Him in faith, asking for His blessing and trusting in His limitless power, He is able to grant us increase beyond what we can imagine.

The testimony of Jabez encourages us to pray bold prayers and to believe that God can expand our territory, whether that means influence, opportunities, or impact, when we trust Him. It reminds us that God is a God of abundance, not lack, and that His ability to bless and multiply our lives is without limit.

Modern-Day Testimonies of God's Limitless Possibilities

God's limitless possibilities are not confined to the pages of the Bible. Even today, there are countless testimonies of people who have experienced the miraculous power of God's multiplication, provision, and healing in their lives. These modern-day stories serve as a reminder that God is still working in extraordinary ways and that His promises are as true today as they were in biblical times.

One such testimony is the story of a missionary couple who were serving in a remote village in Africa. The couple had limited resources and often struggled to meet the needs of the people they were ministering to. One day, they were faced with a particularly challenging situation, a local family was in desperate need of food, but the couple had very little to give. They decided to share the small amount of food they had with the family, trusting that God would somehow provide.

As they distributed the food, something miraculous happened. No matter how much they gave, the food never ran out. What started as a small meal was multiplied in their hands, allowing them to feed not only the family in need but also several others in the village. This modern-day miracle of multiplication is a powerful testimony of God's limitless possibilities and His ability to provide in ways that defy natural explanation.

Another modern testimony comes from a woman who had been struggling with a severe illness for many years. Despite seeing numerous doctors and trying various treatments, her condition continued to worsen. In desperation, she attended a healing service at her church, where she was prayed for by the elders. Though there was no immediate change, the woman continued to pray and trust God for her healing.

Months later, she went for a routine check-up and was astonished to learn that her illness had completely disappeared. The doctors had no explanation for her sudden recovery, but the woman knew that it was the result of God's healing power. Her testimony is a powerful reminder that God's possibilities are limitless, even when medical science has no answers.

These testimonies, both biblical and modern, showcase the incredible, limitless possibilities that arise when we trust in God's compound interest and His ability to multiply our small acts of faith. God is not limited by our circumstances, resources, or time. When we place our trust in Him, He works in ways that go far beyond anything we could ever imagine, bringing about miraculous breakthroughs, provision, healing, and increase.

CHAPTER 6

THE ROLE OF PRAYER AND PROPHETIC DECLARATIONS

Prayer is one of the most powerful tools that God has given us as believers. It is our direct line of communication with the Creator of the universe, the means by which we align ourselves with His will, and the way in which we access the resources of heaven to affect change on earth. But prayer is not just about speaking words; it is about engaging with God in a way that brings about spiritual results. When we pray effectively, we activate the power of heaven to work on our behalf, and we see the spiritual realities of God's promises manifest in our lives.

In addition to prayer, prophetic declaration, which is speaking forth God's word over our lives and circumstances, plays a vital role in unlocking the supernatural. Through both prayer and prophetic declarations, we move beyond the natural realm into the spiritual, where limitless possibilities unfold.

To engage in effective prayer, we must first understand what prayer truly is. At its centre, prayer is communion with God, an intimate exchange where we communicate our hearts, listen to His voice, and align our desires with His will. It is not simply a religious ritual or a list of requests; rather, it is a conversation with the One who holds all power and authority.

James 5:16 says, "The effective, fervent prayer of a righteous man avails much." This verse reveals that prayer can be powerful and effective, but it also indicates that not all prayer yields the same results. There is a difference between casual or routine prayers and prayers that produce spiritual breakthroughs. Effective prayer is marked by passion, focus, faith, and persistence. It is rooted in the righteousness that comes through a relationship with Jesus Christ and is driven by the desire to see God's will come to pass.

The Power of Persistence in Prayer

One of the keys to effective prayer is persistence. Jesus Himself emphasized the importance of persistence in prayer through the parable of the persistent widow in Luke 18:1-8. In this parable, a widow persistently brought her case before an unjust judge, seeking justice against her adversary. Though the judge initially refused to help her, he eventually relented because of her persistence.

Jesus used this parable to teach His disciples the importance of never giving up in prayer. He said, "And shall God not avenge His own elect who cry out day and night to Him, though He bears long with them? I tell you that He will avenge them speedily" (Luke 18:7-8). Jesus wanted to convey that if even an unjust judge would eventually act because of persistence, how much more will our righteous and loving Father respond when we persist in prayer?

Persistence in prayer demonstrates faith. It shows that we believe God is both willing and able to answer, even when we don't see immediate results. It is easy to become discouraged when our prayers aren't answered right away, but effective prayer requires that we continue to press in, trusting that God hears us and will answer in His perfect timing. In Matthew 7:7, Jesus tells us, "Ask, and it will be given to you; seek, and you will find; knock, and it will be opened to you." The verbs in this verse are present continuous, meaning that we should keep asking, keep seeking, and keep knocking until we receive an answer.

Praying in Alignment with God's Will

For our prayers to be effective, they must be aligned with God's will. Prayer is not about imposing our will on God or trying to convince Him to do what we want. Rather, it is about coming into agreement with His will and allowing His desires to shape our prayers. When we pray in alignment with God's will, we can have confidence that He will answer, because we are asking for what He already desires to give.

1 John 5:14-15 says, "Now this is the confidence that we have in Him, that if we ask anything according to His will, He hears us. And if we know that He hears us, whatever we ask, we know that we have the petitions that we have asked of Him." This passage assures us that when we pray in alignment with God's will, we can be confident that He hears us and will grant our requests.

The question, then, is how do we discern God's will in prayer? The primary way we align our prayers with God's will is through His word. The Bible reveals God's heart, His character, and His promises. As we study Scripture and meditate on His word, our hearts and minds are transformed, and we begin to desire what He desires. Praying the word of God is one of the most powerful ways to ensure that our prayers are in alignment with His will. When we declare His promises and speak His truth over our lives, we are praying in agreement with heaven.

Another way to discern God's will in prayer is through the guidance of the Holy Spirit. Romans 8:26-27 tells us, "Likewise the Spirit also helps in our weaknesses. For we do not know what we should pray for as we ought, but the Spirit Himself makes intercession for us with groanings which cannot be uttered. Now He who searches the hearts knows what the mind of the Spirit is, because He makes intercession for the saints according to the will of God."

The Holy Spirit is our helper in prayer, guiding us when we don't know what to pray. He intercedes on our behalf, praying in alignment with God's will even when we cannot find the words. This is why it is essential to develop a relationship with the Holy Spirit in our prayer lives. By listening to His promptings and allowing Him to lead our prayers, we can be confident that we are praying according to God's will.

The Role of Faith in Effective Prayer

Faith is a critical component of effective prayer. Hebrews 11:6 tells us, "But without faith it is impossible to please Him, for he who comes to God must believe that He is, and that He is a rewarder of those who diligently seek Him." Faith is the assurance that God hears us, that He is able to answer, and that He is faithful to fulfill His promises. Without faith, our prayers are empty words, but when we pray in faith, we activate the power of God to move in our lives.

Jesus often emphasized the importance of faith in prayer. In Mark 11:24, He said, "Therefore I say to you, whatever things you ask when you pray, believe that you receive them, and you will have them." This scripture shows the connection between prayer and faith, when we pray, we must believe that we have already received the answer, even if we don't see it yet in the natural. This kind of faith is not based on our circumstances or feelings but on the unchanging nature of God and His promises.

Faith is what enables us to pray with confidence, knowing that God is both willing and able to answer. However, faith is not merely positive thinking or wishful hope. Biblical faith is rooted in a deep trust in God's character and His word. It is the assurance that He is who He says He is and that He will do what He has promised.

The Bible is filled with examples of individuals who experienced powerful results through faith-filled prayer. One such example is the story of the centurion in Matthew 8:5-13. The centurion came to Jesus, asking Him to heal his servant, but when Jesus offered to come to his house, the centurion replied, "Lord, I am not worthy that You should come under my roof. But only speak a word, and my servant will be healed" (Matthew 8:8).

Jesus marveled at the centurion's faith and said, "Go your way; and as you have believed, so let it be done for you" (Matthew 8:13). The centurion's faith in Jesus' ability to heal, even from a distance, resulted in the immediate healing of his servant. This story illustrates that when we pray with faith, we open the door for God's power to manifest in our lives in extraordinary ways.

Engaging in Effective Prayer and Prophetic Declarations

To engage in effective prayer and prophetic declarations, here are some practical steps:

Pray the Word of God: One of the most powerful ways to ensure that your prayers are aligned with God's will is to pray His Word. Find Scriptures that apply to your situation and pray them back to God, trusting that He will honor His promises.

Speak Life: Be mindful of the words you speak over yourself and your circumstances. Avoid negative or doubt-filled speech, and instead, declare God's truth and promises with faith.

Persist in Prayer: Don't give up if you don't see immediate results. Keep asking, seeking, and knocking, knowing that God is faithful to answer in His perfect timing.

Listen to the Holy Spirit: Allow the Holy Spirit to guide your prayers and prophetic declarations. Be sensitive to His leading and trust that He will direct you to pray and speak according to God's will.

Believe in the Power of Your Words: Remember that your words carry power. When you make prophetic declarations, do so with faith, knowing that you are partnering with God to release His will on earth.

The Power of Prophetic Declarations and Speaking Life

Words have tremendous power. The Bible emphasizes the significance of the words we speak and how they can shape our reality. Proverbs 18:21 declares, "Death and life are in the power of the tongue, and those who love it will eat its fruit." This means that our words have the ability to bring life or death to our circumstances, relationships, and spiritual well-being. Prophetic declarations are a form of using this power, speaking forth God's word and His promises into our lives, situations, and the world around us.

When we engage in prophetic declarations, we partner with God to release His will on earth. We align our speech with His word, and as we speak life, we activate the spiritual realm to bring about transformation. Prophetic declarations are not mere positive affirmations; they are Spirit-led proclamations rooted in the authority of God's Word and fueled by faith.

Prophetic declarations are bold, faith-filled statements in which we declare God's truth over our lives and circumstances. They are based on the belief that God's word is alive and active, capable of producing results. Hebrews 4:12 tells us, "For the word of God is living and powerful, and sharper than any two-edged sword." When we declare God's Word, we release its power to accomplish what He has spoken.

Prophetic declarations are particularly powerful because they tap into the authority that God has given us as believers. Jesus said in Matthew 18:18, "Assuredly, I say to you, whatever you bind on earth will be bound in heaven, and whatever you loose on earth will be loosed in heaven." This means that we have the authority to speak into situations and see heaven's will come to pass on earth. When we declare God's Word, we are exercising the authority that Jesus has given us to bind the enemy's plans and release God's purposes.

The words we speak carry authority in the spiritual realm. Just as God spoke the universe into existence with His words (Genesis 1), we also have the power to shape our world through our speech. When we declare life, healing, provision, and breakthrough according to God's Word, we set in motion the spiritual forces necessary to bring those things to pass.

Examples of Prophetic Declarations in Scripture

Throughout the Bible, we find numerous examples of individuals who made prophetic declarations and saw powerful results. These examples illustrate that speaking life through declarations of faith can bring about miraculous changes in seemingly impossible situations.

Ezekiel and the Valley of Dry Bones

One of the most dramatic examples of the power of prophetic declarations is found in Ezekiel 37, where the prophet Ezekiel is led by the Spirit of the Lord to a valley full of dry bones. God asks Ezekiel, "Son of man, can these bones live?" (Ezekiel 37:3). Ezekiel responds by deferring to God's knowledge, saying, "O Lord God, You know."

God then commands Ezekiel to prophesy to the bones. He tells Ezekiel to speak life into the bones, declaring that they will live again. As Ezekiel begins to prophesy, something miraculous happens: the bones start to come together, tendons and flesh form on them, and the breath of life enters them. What was once a valley of death is transformed into a living army through the power of prophetic declarations.

This story is a powerful reminder that when we declare God's word over seemingly dead or hopeless situations, we invite His resurrection power to bring life. Ezekiel's declaration didn't come from his own ideas or strength; it was based on the Word of the Lord. Likewise, when we make prophetic declarations, they must be rooted in what God has spoken, not in our own desires or opinions. As we align our words with His, we release His power to transform situations, no matter how impossible they may seem.

Jesus' Declarations of Healing and Deliverance

Throughout His ministry, Jesus consistently demonstrated the power of speaking life through prophetic declarations. One such example is found in Mark 4:39, when Jesus and His disciples were caught in a violent storm on the Sea of Galilee. As the disciples feared for their lives, Jesus stood up and declared, "Peace, be still!" Immediately, the wind ceased, and there was a great calm.

In this instance, Jesus didn't pray a long, drawn-out prayer. He simply made a declaration of peace, and the natural elements responded to His words. This shows us that prophetic declarations don't always have to be lengthy or complicated. Sometimes, a simple statement spoken in faith can bring about powerful results. Jesus' authority over the storm is the same authority He has given us as His followers. When we speak life into our circumstances with faith, we can expect the supernatural to manifest.

Another example of Jesus using prophetic declarations is in John 11:43, when He raised Lazarus from the dead. After Lazarus had been in the tomb for four days, Jesus arrived and declared, "Lazarus, come forth!" At His word, Lazarus was resurrected and walked out of the grave. This miracle demonstrates the life-giving power of prophetic declarations. Just as Jesus called Lazarus out of death and into life, we too can declare life over situations that seem dead, believing that God's Word has the power to bring about resurrection and restoration.

David's Declaration of Victory Over Goliath

The story of David and Goliath in 1 Samuel 17 provides another example of the power of prophetic declarations. Before David went into battle against the giant Goliath, he made a bold declaration of victory: "This day the Lord will deliver you into my hand, and I will strike you and take your head from you" (1 Samuel 17:46). David's declaration was not based on his own ability or strength but on his faith in God's power to deliver him.

As David spoke, he released the power of God into the situation, and the battle was won before it even began. His prophetic declaration paved the way for the victory that followed. This story reminds us that when we declare God's promises over our battles, we are positioning ourselves for victory. Our declarations of faith align us with God's plans, allowing His power to flow through us and bring about the outcome He desires.

The Impact of Speaking Life

When we make prophetic declarations, we are engaging in spiritual warfare, speaking life into our circumstances, and partnering with God to bring about His will. This principle is evident in Proverbs 18:21, which teaches that "death and life are in the power of the tongue." Our words carry the ability to bring forth life or death, healing or harm, blessings or curses. This is why it is so important to be mindful of the words we speak, not only in prayer but in our everyday conversations.

When we speak life, we are sowing seeds of faith that can produce a harvest of blessings in our lives and the lives of others. Speaking life means declaring God's truth over ourselves, our families, our communities, and our futures. It means refusing to speak words of doubt, fear, or negativity, and instead choosing to speak words that align with God's promises.

In James 3:5-6, the Bible compares the tongue to a small fire that can set an entire forest ablaze. This imagery highlights the significant impact that our words can have, both for good and for bad. Just as a small spark can cause a large fire, so too can our words ignite powerful spiritual results. When we speak life, we are setting in motion the forces of heaven to bring about God's purposes in our lives.

Declaring Life Over Ourselves

One of the most important areas where we need to speak life is over ourselves. Many people struggle with negative self-talk, speaking words of doubt, fear, or failure over their own lives. However, as believers, we are called to declare God's truth over ourselves. This means speaking His promises, not our insecurities or weaknesses.

When we declare life over ourselves, we are affirming our identity in Christ. We are declaring that we are more than conquerors through Him (Romans 8:37), that we are fearfully and wonderfully made (Psalm 139:14), and that we have been given everything we need for life and godliness (2 Peter 1:3). These declarations not only reinforce our faith but also align our minds with God's truth, transforming how we see ourselves and our circumstances.

Speaking life over ourselves also involves declaring victory over the battles we face. Whether it's a battle with sickness, financial hardship, or emotional struggles, we have the power to declare God's promises of healing, provision, and peace. In Isaiah 55:11, God says, "So shall My word be that goes forth from My mouth; it shall not return to Me void, but it shall accomplish what I please, and it shall prosper in the thing for which I sent it." When we declare His Word, we can be confident that it will accomplish what He has spoken.

Declaring Life Over Others

In addition to declaring life over ourselves, we are called to speak life into the lives of others. This could be our family members, friends, coworkers, or even strangers. Our words have the power to encourage, uplift, and bring healing to those around us. Ephesians 4:29 instructs us, "Let no corrupt word proceed out of your mouth, but what is good for necessary edification, that it may impart grace to the hearers."

Speaking life over others means choosing to see them through God's eyes and declaring His truth over their lives. This might involve encouraging someone who is struggling, speaking words of blessing over a friend or family member, or even making prophetic declarations over a situation that seems hopeless. When we speak life, we are partnering with God to release His grace and favor into the lives of those around us.

One powerful example of speaking life over others is found in the ministry of apostle Paul. In his letters to the early churches, Paul often spoke prophetic blessings and declarations over the believers. In Ephesians 1:17-18, he declares, "That the God of our Lord Jesus Christ, the Father of glory, may give to you the spirit of wisdom and revelation in the knowledge of Him, the eyes of your understanding being enlightened." Paul's declarations over the early believers were designed to release spiritual insight, wisdom, and blessing into their lives.

We too have the ability to release blessings through our words. Whether it's praying over our children, declaring healing over a sick friend, or speaking encouragement to someone in need, our words can bring life and hope to those around us.

How to Make Effective Prophetic Declarations

To make effective prophetic declarations, here are a few practical steps:

Root Your Declarations in God's Word: The most powerful declarations are those that are based on Scripture. When we declare God's promises, we are speaking His truth, which carries authority and power.

Speak with Faith and Boldness: Prophetic declarations require faith. When you declare life, do so with the confidence that God will bring it to pass. Speak with boldness, knowing that your words have power in the spiritual realm.

Be Consistent: Prophetic declarations are not a one-time event. Be consistent in declaring God's truth over your life and circumstances. Even when you don't see immediate results, continue to declare His promises, trusting that they will come to pass.

Listen to the Holy Spirit: Allow the Holy Spirit to guide your declarations. Sometimes, He will prompt you to declare specific things over a situation or a person. Be sensitive to His leading, and trust that He knows exactly what needs to be spoken.

Speak Life in All Circumstances: Whether you're facing a battle, walking through a season of waiting, or experiencing a breakthrough, always choose to speak life. Let your words reflect God's promises, even in the most challenging situations.

The power of prophetic declarations lies in the fact that our words, when aligned with God's will, can bring life, healing, and transformation. When we declare God's promises over our lives, we are releasing the authority of heaven to work on our behalf. Whether we are speaking life over ourselves, others, or situations, prophetic declarations are a powerful tool that God has given us to shape our reality according to His Word.

As we continue to engage in prayer and prophetic declarations, we will see the spiritual results of speaking life. We will witness God's promises being fulfilled, breakthroughs in areas of difficulty, and transformation in both our lives and the lives of those around us. Let us be mindful of the power of our words and use them to declare God's truth and release His will on earth.

CHAPTER 7

PRACTICAL STEPS FOR DAILY PROPHETIC ACTIVATION

S tarting your day with purpose and spiritual intentionality is one of the most powerful things you can do to set the tone for the rest of your day. When you activate your day with prayer, prophetic declarations, and the presence of God, you position yourself to walk in alignment with His will and experience divine favor, guidance, and breakthrough. Rather than allowing the pressures and challenges of life to dictate how your day unfolds, prophetic activation empowers you to take charge of your spiritual atmosphere and invite God's power to operate in every aspect of your life.

Let's look at practical steps you can take each morning to activate your day prophetically. By following these steps, you will not only invite God's presence into your daily life but also release the authority and power He has given you to shape your day according to His will.

The Importance of Daily Prophetic Activation

Before diving into the practical steps for activating your day, it's important to understand why daily prophetic activation is so essential. As believers, we are in a constant spiritual battle. Ephesians 6:12 reminds us, "For we do not wrestle against flesh and blood, but against principalities, against powers, against the rulers of the darkness of this age, against spiritual hosts of wickedness in the heavenly places." The spiritual realm is always at work, and the enemy's goal is to disrupt, discourage, and distract us from fulfilling God's purpose.

Daily prophetic activation helps us proactively engage with the spiritual realm rather than reactively responding to the enemy's attacks. By beginning each day in prayer, worship, and prophetic declarations, we equip ourselves with the spiritual armor to walk in victory. We also align ourselves with God's plans and purposes, ensuring that we move in step with His will throughout the day.

Additionally, prophetic activation helps us to be spiritually sensitive and aware of God's presence and leading. It sharpens our discernment, allowing us to recognize His voice and respond to His promptings. As we consistently activate our day, we cultivate an atmosphere where miracles, breakthroughs, and divine intervention become a natural part of our daily lives.

Step 1: Begin With Gratitude And Worship

The first step to activating your day is to enter into God's presence with a heart of gratitude and worship. Psalm 100:4 says, "Enter into His gates with thanksgiving, and into His courts with praise. Be thankful to Him, and bless His name." Gratitude and worship are powerful spiritual tools that help to shift our focus from ourselves and our problems to God and His goodness. When we start our day by thanking God for who He is and what He has done, we cultivate a mindset of faith and expectation.

Worship also creates an atmosphere for God's presence to manifest. In John 4:23-24, Jesus explains that "the true worshipers will worship the Father in spirit and truth; for the Father is seeking such to worship Him." When we worship, we are expressing our love and adoration for God and creating an environment where He can dwell and work. Worship invites the presence of God into our lives, and where His presence is, there is fullness of joy, peace, and power (Psalm 16:11).

Practical steps to begin your day with gratitude and worship include:

Take a moment to thank God for a new day: As soon as you wake up, express gratitude to God for giving you life, health, and strength to face a new day. Thank Him for His faithfulness, His provision, and His love.

Play worship music: Whether you prefer a quiet instrumental or an upbeat song, playing worship music can help set the tone for your morning. As you listen to the music, allow your heart to engage in worship and lift the name of Jesus.

Speak out your thanksgiving: Verbalize your gratitude to God by thanking Him for specific blessings. This could be for your family, your job, your health, or anything else you are grateful for. When you speak out your thanks, you shift the spiritual atmosphere and open the door for more of God's goodness to flow into your day.

Step 2: Engage In Focused Prayer

After beginning your day with gratitude and worship, the next step is to engage in focused prayer. Prayer is the foundation of prophetic activation because it is through prayer that we communicate with God, receive His guidance, and align ourselves with His will. Effective prayer in the morning sets the spiritual direction for the rest of your day.

Jesus modeled the importance of early morning prayer during His time on earth. In Mark 1:35, we read that "in the morning, having risen a long while before daylight, He went out and departed to a solitary place, and there He prayed." Jesus understood the importance of starting the day in communion with the Father, and if it was essential for Him, how much more should it be for us?

During this time of focused prayer, there are several key areas to cover:

Pray for Divine Guidance: Ask God to lead and guide you throughout the day. Proverbs 3:5-6 encourages us to "trust in the Lord with all your heart, and lean not on your understanding; in all your ways acknowledge Him, and He shall direct your paths." Pray for God's wisdom, discernment, and clarity as you make decisions and encounter various daily situations.

Pray for Protection: Pray for God's protection for yourself, your family, and your loved ones. Psalm 91 is a powerful passage to declare over your life each morning. Pray for God's angels to surround you and guard you from any attacks or schemes of the enemy.

Pray for Opportunities to Be a Blessing: Ask God to open doors for you to be a vessel of His love, grace, and truth to others. Whether through acts of kindness, sharing the gospel, or offering encouragement, pray that God will give you opportunities to shine His light in the lives of those you encounter.

Pray in the Spirit: If you have the gift of speaking in tongues, pray in the Spirit. Romans 8:26 tells us that "the Spirit also helps in our weaknesses. For we do not know what we should pray for as we ought, but the Spirit Himself makes intercession for us with groanings which cannot be uttered." Praying in the Spirit allows you to pray in alignment with God's will, even when you don't know what to pray for.

Step 3: Make Prophetic Declarations

Prophetic declarations are a vital component of daily prophetic activation. After praying, declare God's promises and truth over your day. As discussed in the previous chapter, prophetic declarations are powerful because they release God's will into the natural realm. When you declare His Word with faith, you align your circumstances with His promises and activate God's supernatural power.

Some examples of prophetic declarations you can make each morning include:

Declaring God's Favor: "Today, I declare that I am walking in the favor of God. Doors of opportunity are opening for me, and I am blessed in everything I do. The favor of God surrounds me like a shield, and I will experience success and breakthroughs in every area of my life."

Declaring God's Protection: "I declare that no weapon formed against me shall prosper. The Lord is my refuge and fortress, and His angels are encamped around me. I am safe under the shadow of the Almighty, and no harm will come near my dwelling."

Declaring Victory Over Challenges: "I declare that I am more than a conqueror through Christ who loves me. No matter what challenges or obstacles I face today, I will overcome them with the power of God. I walk in victory, and I am not defeated."

Declaring Divine Health and Healing: "I declare that by the stripes of Jesus, I am healed. Every part of my body functions in divine order, and I walk in supernatural health. Sickness and disease have no place in my life, and I am strong and healthy in Jesus' name."

Declaring Provision: "I declare that God supplies all my needs according to His riches in glory. Lack is not my portion, and I live in abundance. I have enough to fulfill my purpose and bless others."

These declarations are not merely positive affirmations; they are based on the authority of God's word. As you make these declarations in faith, you speak life into your circumstances and position yourself to experience God's best.

Step 4: Meditate On God's Word

Meditating on God's word is another essential step in activating your day. Joshua 1:8 tells us, "This Book of the Law shall not depart from your mouth, but you shall meditate in it day and night, that you may observe to do according to all written in it. For then you will make your way prosperous, and then you will have success."

Meditating on God's word allows it to take root in your heart and shape your thinking. This is crucial for prophetic activation because the Word of God is the foundation of everything we believe and declare. By starting your day with Scripture, you align your thoughts with God's truth and equip yourself to face any challenges that may come.

Some practical ways to meditate on God's word each morning include:

Read a Passage of Scripture: Choose a passage of Scripture to read and reflect on. You might follow a Bible reading plan, study a particular book, or focus on a specific theme, such as faith, healing, or God's promises.

Reflect on a Key Verse: After reading a passage, choose one verse that stands out and meditate on it throughout the day. Consider what the verse reveals about God's character, how it applies to your life, and how you can put it into practice.

Journal Your Reflections: Writing down your thoughts and insights from your Bible reading can help you process and internalize God's Word. Journaling also allows you to look back and see how God has spoken to you over time.

Memorize Scripture: Memorizing Scripture is a powerful way to carry God's Word throughout the day. Choose one verse each week to memorize, and recite it during your morning routine or throughout the day.

Step 5: Commit Your Day To God

The final step in activating your day is committing everything to God's hands. Proverbs 16:3 says, "Commit your works to the Lord, and your thoughts will be established." After praying, worship, prophetic declarations, and the Word, take a moment to surrender your day to God. Acknowledge that He is in control and that you trust Him to guide you in every decision, conversation, and situation.

This act of surrender not only invites God to take the lead in your day, but it also brings peace and confidence, knowing that He is working all things together for your good (Romans 8:28). When you commit your day to God, you are placing your trust in His ability to order your steps and bring about His purpose in your life.

Practical ways to commit your day to God include:

Pray for His Will to Be Done: As you wrap up your morning activation, pray for God's will to be done in every area of your life. Ask Him to align your desires, actions, and plans with His purpose.

Trust Him with Your Schedule: Commit your to-do list, meetings, and responsibilities to God. Ask Him to give you wisdom and strength to accomplish what needs to be done and to prioritize what matters most.

Invite the Holy Spirit to Lead You: Ask the Holy Spirit to guide you throughout the day. Be sensitive to His leading, whether through a gentle nudge, a word of encouragement, or an opportunity to minister to someone.

Daily prophetic activation is a powerful practice that equips you to walk in spiritual victory. By beginning your day with gratitude, focused prayer, prophetic declarations, and meditation on God's Word, you create an atmosphere for God's presence to move in your life. These practical steps not only position you to receive God's guidance, protection, and favor but also empower you to speak life and declare His promises over your circumstances.

You will grow in spiritual sensitivity, authority, and confidence as you consistently activate your day. You will be equipped to face challenges with faith, overcome obstacles with victory, and experience the fullness of God's power and purpose in your life. Commit to making daily prophetic activation a part of your morning routine, and watch how God transforms your life through the power of His presence and word.

Practical Steps To Remain Consistent In Spiritual Growth

One of the most significant challenges many believers face is maintaining consistency in their spiritual growth. Just as physical growth requires proper nutrition, exercise, and discipline, spiritual growth also demands intentionality, commitment, and persistence. While seasons of rapid spiritual growth are exhilarating, there are also seasons when we may feel stagnant or face spiritual opposition that makes consistency difficult. However, maintaining steady, continual growth is essential for deepening our relationship with God, developing spiritual maturity, and fulfilling our God-given purpose.

Let's examine practical steps that will help you remain consistent in your spiritual growth. These steps are designed to keep you grounded in your faith, focused on your spiritual journey, and aligned with God's plan for your life. By implementing these practices regularly, you can create a sustainable rhythm of spiritual growth that will carry you through both the highs and lows of life.

Step 1: Develop A Daily Routine
Of Spiritual Disciplines

One of the most effective ways to remain consistent in spiritual growth is to establish a daily routine of spiritual disciplines. Spiritual disciplines, such as prayer, Bible study, worship, fasting, and meditation, are practices that help us draw closer to God and grow in our faith. These disciplines are not merely religious duties; they are opportunities to connect with God on a deeper level and receive the spiritual nourishment we need for growth.

To develop a consistent routine, begin by identifying the spiritual disciplines that resonate most with you and align with your spiritual goals. For example, if your goal is to deepen your understanding of Scripture, you might prioritize daily Bible study and meditation. If your goal is to strengthen your prayer life, you might set aside dedicated time each day for focused prayer and intercession.

Here are some practical tips for establishing a daily routine of spiritual disciplines:

Set a specific time for spiritual activities: Consistency often depends on routine. Set aside a specific time each day for spiritual disciplines, whether it's in the morning, during lunch breaks, or before bed. Having a set time helps to form a habit and ensures that you are prioritizing your spiritual growth.

Create a dedicated space for prayer and study: Having a specific location where you meet with God can help create a sense of sacredness and focus. Whether it's a quiet corner of your home or a specific chair in your room, choose a place that is free from distractions and conducive to worship and reflection.

Start small and build gradually: If you're new to spiritual disciplines, it's important to start small and build up gradually.

Instead of trying to engage in hours of prayer or Bible study right away, start with a manageable amount of time (e.g., 15-30 minutes) and gradually increase it as you grow more comfortable.

Be flexible: While consistency is important, life's circumstances may occasionally disrupt your routine. Be flexible and give yourself grace when things don't go as planned. The key is to maintain a general rhythm, even if it looks different on some days.

Step 2: Surround Yourself With A Community Of Believers

Spiritual growth is not something we are meant to pursue in isolation. God designed us to grow in the context of community, where we can be encouraged, challenged, and supported by fellow believers. Hebrews 10:24-25 exhorts us, "And let us consider one another in order to stir up love and good works, not forsaking the assembling of ourselves together, as is the manner of some, but exhorting one another, and so much the more as you see the Day approaching."

Being part of a community of believers helps us stay accountable in our spiritual journey and provides opportunities for growth through fellowship, teaching, and mutual encouragement. Whether it's attending church services, joining a small group, or participating in Bible study classes, surrounding yourself with others who are also pursuing spiritual growth can help you stay motivated and consistent.

Here are some practical ways to engage with a community of believers:

Join a small group or Bible study: Small groups provide a more intimate setting for fellowship, discussion, and prayer. They allow you to build meaningful relationships with others who can support you in your spiritual journey.

Attend church services regularly: Regular church attendance is important for receiving spiritual teaching, worshiping corporately, and connecting with the broader body of Christ. Make it a priority to attend services consistently, and seek ways to serve and contribute to your church community.

Find a spiritual mentor or accountability partner: Having someone who can offer guidance, wisdom, and encouragement is invaluable for spiritual growth. A mentor or accountability partner can pray with you, offer counsel, and help keep you on track when you face challenges.

Participate in Christian events or conferences: Attending Christian conferences, retreats, or workshops can provide a spiritual boost and equip you with tools for growth. These events often feature powerful teaching, worship, and fellowship that can inspire and renew your commitment to God.

Step 3: Feed Your Spirit With The Word Of God

Just as our bodies need food to grow, our spirits need to be nourished with the Word of God. Jesus said in Matthew 4:4, "Man shall not live by bread alone, but by every word that proceeds from the mouth of God." Consistently feeding on Scripture is crucial for spiritual growth because it provides the foundation for everything we believe and practice as followers of Christ.

The Bible not only teaches us about God's character and His promises but also serves as a guide for how to live in alignment with His will. As you read and study Scripture, you will find your faith strengthened, your mind renewed, and your spirit transformed. Consistent Bible reading and study should be a central part of your daily spiritual routine.

Here are some practical tips for feeding your spirit with the word of God:

Follow a Bible reading plan: If you struggle with knowing where to start in your Bible reading, consider following a Bible reading plan. These plans offer a structured approach to reading through the Bible in a year, focusing on specific books, or exploring particular themes.

Use a study Bible or commentary: To gain a deeper understanding of Scripture, use a study Bible or a Bible commentary that provides explanations, historical context, and theological insights. This will help you go beyond surface-level reading and engage more deeply with the text.

Memorize Scripture: Memorizing key verses helps you internalize God's Word and carry it with you throughout the day. Choose a verse each week to memorize and meditate on, and find creative ways to incorporate it into your daily life.

Journal your reflections: Journaling can be a powerful tool for processing what you are learning in Scripture. As you read, write down any insights, questions, or applications that stand out to you. This practice helps you engage more thoughtfully with the Word and allows you to look back and track your spiritual growth over time.

Step 4: Engage In Regular Self-Reflection And Evaluation

To remain consistent in your spiritual growth, it's important to regularly evaluate your progress and reflect on where you are in your walk with God. Just as an athlete or professional regularly assesses their performance to improve, we too must take time to assess our spiritual condition and growth. This practice of self-reflection helps us identify areas where we are growing, areas where we may be stagnant, and areas where we need to make adjustments.

Psalm 139:23-24 says, "Search me, O God, and know my heart; try me, and know my anxieties; and see if there is any wicked way in me, and lead me in the way everlasting." Regular self-reflection invites God to search our hearts and reveal anything that may be hindering our growth or drawing us away from Him.

Here are some practical ways to engage in regular self-reflection and evaluation:

Set aside time for personal reflection: Schedule regular times (e.g., weekly or monthly) to reflect on your spiritual journey. Ask yourself questions such as: "Am I growing closer to God?" "Am I consistently engaging in spiritual disciplines?" "What areas of my life need more attention?"

Examine your heart: Reflect on the condition of your heart, including your attitudes, motivations, and desires. Are you living in alignment with God's will? Are there any areas of pride, bitterness, or fear that need to be surrendered to Him?

Evaluate your spiritual habits: Take an honest look at your spiritual habits and routines. Are you spending enough time in prayer, Bible study, and worship? Are there any areas where you need to make adjustments to stay consistent?

Set spiritual goals: Setting specific, measurable spiritual goals can help you stay focused and intentional in your growth. For example, you might set a goal to read through the New Testament in a certain time frame, memorize a set number of Scriptures, or engage in a particular ministry or service opportunity.

Step 5: Stay Persistent In The Face Of Challenges

Consistency in spiritual growth doesn't mean that you won't face challenges along the way. In fact, spiritual growth often attracts opposition from the enemy, as he seeks to hinder your progress and cause you to give up. However, remaining persistent in the face of challenges is key to continued growth.

James 1:2-4 encourages us, "My brethren, count it all joy when you fall into various trials, knowing that the testing of your faith produces patience. But let patience have its perfect work, that you may be perfect and complete, lacking nothing." Trials and difficulties are opportunities for growth, and if we remain persistent, we will come out stronger and more mature in our faith.

Here are some practical tips for staying persistent when challenges arise:

Lean on God's strength: When you face challenges, rely on God's strength rather than your own. Philippians 4:13 reminds us, "I can do all things through Christ who strengthens me." Spend extra time in prayer and worship, asking God for the grace and strength to persevere.

Seek support from others: Don't try to face challenges alone. Reach out to your church community, small group, or spiritual mentor for prayer, encouragement, and support. Others can help bear your burdens and provide wisdom when you feel overwhelmed.

Remind yourself of God's promises: When challenges come, remind yourself of God's promises. Reflect on Scriptures that speak of His faithfulness, protection, and provision, and declare those promises over your life. God has promised never to leave or forsake you (Hebrews 13:5), and His Word will not return void (Isaiah 55:11).

Keep your eyes on the long-term goal: Spiritual growth is a lifelong journey, and consistency requires a long-term perspective. When challenges come, keep your focus on the ultimate goal of becoming more like Christ and fulfilling His purpose for your life. Trust that God is using every difficulty to shape you and draw you closer to Him.

Step 6: Develop a Heart of Humility and Dependence on God

Finally, to remain consistent in spiritual growth, it's essential to cultivate a heart of humility and dependence on God. Spiritual growth is not something we can achieve through our own efforts; it is a work of the Holy Spirit in us. As we grow, we must continually acknowledge our need for God's grace, guidance, and power.

John 15:5 reminds us of the importance of abiding in Christ: "I am the vine, you are the branches. He who abides in Me, and I in him, bears much fruit; for without Me you can do nothing." Staying connected to Christ through prayer, worship, and His Word is the only way to produce lasting spiritual fruit. As we remain humble and dependent on God, we open ourselves up to the continual work of the Holy Spirit in our lives.

Here are some practical ways to cultivate humility and dependence on God:

Acknowledge your need for God daily: Begin each day by acknowledging your dependence on God. Pray for His guidance, strength, and grace to carry you through the day.

Surrender your plans and desires: Regularly surrender your plans, desires, and ambitions to God, asking Him to align your heart with His will. Be willing to let go of anything that is hindering your spiritual growth.

Invite the Holy Spirit to lead you: Ask the Holy Spirit to fill you each day and to lead you in every decision and action. Trust that He is working in you to bring about God's purposes (Philippians 2:13).

CONCLUSION

Walking In The Manifestation
Of God's Limitless Power

A s we conclude this book, it is important to remember that the principles you have learned are not just one-time strategies but daily practices that, when consistently applied, will allow you to live a life marked by the manifestation of God's limitless power. Walking in spiritual authority, activating your day with intentional prayer, and speaking life through prophetic declarations are foundational to experiencing God's presence and power in every area of your life.

The life God has called you to is not one of defeat, fear, or stagnation. He has called you to live in victory, to walk in purpose, and to be a vessel through which His kingdom is advanced on earth. The power of God is available to you not only in moments of crisis but in the everyday rhythms of life. The key is learning to consistently tap into that power through the principles you've discovered in this book. As you continue to grow spiritually and activate your day, you will see the supernatural become a natural part of your life.

One of the most crucial aspects of walking in God's limitless power is the daily activation of your day. Each morning is an opportunity to reset your spiritual focus, realign with God's purposes, and invite His presence to lead you. Every day you have the chance to speak life, declare victory, and set the spiritual tone for the day ahead. As you commit to starting each day with prayer, worship, and prophetic declarations, you are positioning yourself for divine encounters, breakthroughs, and the manifestation of God's promises.

It's important to understand that consistency is key. There will be days when it's difficult to prioritize your spiritual routine, and there may be moments when you don't see immediate results. However, trust that the seeds you are planting through daily activation will bear fruit in due season. Galatians 6:9 reminds us, "And let us not grow weary while doing good, for in due season we shall reap if we do not lose heart." Stay faithful, stay committed, and stay focused, knowing that every step you take to activate your day is bringing you closer to the fulfillment of God's promises in your life.

When challenges arise, and they will, remember that God has already equipped you with everything you need to overcome. You are not fighting for victory; you are fighting from a place of victory because Christ has already won the battle for you. Ephesians 6:10-11 encourages us, "Finally, my brethren, be strong in the Lord and in the power of His might. Put on the whole armor of God, that you may be able to stand against the wiles of the devil." Activating your day is like putting on the armor of God, it prepares you to stand firm in the face of any challenge.

The more you engage in daily activation, the more sensitive you will become to God's leading. You will begin to recognize His voice more clearly, discern His will more accurately, and experience His supernatural intervention in your life. As you continue to activate your day with intentionality, you will find that walking in God's power becomes second nature, and the miraculous becomes a regular occurrence in your life.

Moving Forward in God's Power

As you move forward from this point, understand that God's power is not reserved for a select few or for rare moments of crisis. It is available to every believer who is willing to pursue Him and walk in obedience to His word. The principles you have learned in this book are tools that will help you live a life of spiritual victory, divine favor, and supernatural breakthrough.

As you continue to activate your day, speak life over your circumstances, and trust in God's limitless power, you will experience a life that is not only empowered but also deeply fulfilling. You will find that the ordinary becomes extraordinary when God's presence is invited into every aspect of your life.

Remember, the journey of spiritual growth and walking in God's power is a lifelong process. It is not about perfection, but about continually seeking to grow closer to God and becoming more like Christ each day. There will be ups and downs, but the key is to remain faithful, trusting that God is working in and through you to accomplish His purposes.

As you walk in the manifestation of God's limitless power, know that you are already equipped for victory. The same power that raised Jesus from the dead lives in you (Romans 8:11), and that power is more than enough to overcome any obstacle, fulfill your destiny, and impact the world for God's kingdom.

Be encouraged to continue activating your day with prophetic declarations, bold prayers, and a heart full of faith. Stand firm in the promises of God, knowing that He is faithful to complete the work He has begun in you (Philippians 1:6). As you trust Him, walk in obedience, and speak life into every situation, you will see His power at work in ways that go beyond your imagination.

Walk in the confidence that God is with you, that He is for you, and that He will accomplish great things through you. You are called, chosen, and equipped to live a life of purpose and power. As you continue to pursue Him and activate your day, you will step into the fullness of everything He has prepared for you.

Let your life be a testimony of God's limitless possibilities and His unfailing love. You are destined for victory, and through Christ, all things are possible.

A SPECIAL CALL TO SALVATION & NEW BEGINNINGS FROM APOSTLE DR. DAVID PHILEMON

Dear Beloved,

God loves you deeply and has brought you to this moment for a reason. No matter your past, His love and forgiveness are available to you.

The Bible says in John 3:16, "For God so loved the world that He gave His one and only Son, that whoever believes in Him shall not perish but have eternal life." Jesus Christ came to save you, offering you a new life of purpose and peace.

If you're ready to accept Jesus as your Lord and Savior, pray this simple prayer:

The Salvation Prayer

"Heavenly Father, I come to You in the Name of Jesus. I acknowledge that I am a sinner in need of a Savior. I believe that Jesus Christ is Your Son, that He died for my sins, and that You raised Him from the dead. I repent of my sins and turn to You with my

Whole heart. Jesus, I ask You to come into my life. Be my Lord and my Savior. I surrender my life to You. Fill me with Your Holy Spirit, guide me on the path of righteousness, and help me to follow Your script for my life. Thank you, Father, for saving me. In the name of Jesus. Amen."

Welcome to the Family of God!

If you have just prayed this prayer, Congratulations! You are now a child of God, and heaven is rejoicing. Your journey has begun, and we're here to support you as you grow in faith and discover God's unique plans for you.

Next Steps:
• Connect with a Bible-believing church.
• Read the Bible Daily: God's Word is your guide.
• Pray Regularly: Prayer is your lifeline to God.
• Share Your Faith: Don't keep the good news to yourself.

www.ingramcontent.com/pod-product-compliance
Lightning Source LLC
Chambersburg PA
CBHW060445040426
42331CB00044B/2630